Alfred's GUITAR 101

BOOK 2

AN EXCITING GROUP COURSE FOR ADULTS WHO WANT TO PLAY GUITAR FOR FUN!

TOM DEMPSEY WITH MARTHA MASTERS

Alfred Music
P.O. Box 10003
Van Nuys, CA 91410-0003
alfred.com

Copyright © MMXV by Alfred Music
All rights reserved. Printed in USA.

No part of this book shall be reproduced, arranged, adapted, recorded, publicly performed, stored in a retrieval system, or transmitted by any means without written permission from the publisher. In order to comply with copyright laws, please apply for such written permission and/or license by contacting the publisher at alfred.com/permissions.

ISBN-10: 1-4706-1522-3
ISBN-13: 978-1-4706-1522-2

Cover Art: *View across the Bay*; Juan Gris; Oil on canvas, 1921; Courtesy Wikipaintings.org
Cover photo of Tom Dempsey: Chris Macke / Chris Macke Photography
Cover photo of Martha Masters: Adam Almeida

Table of Contents

GUITAR 101, BOOK 2

Foreword 4

Technique and Reading Music 5

Unit 1: Review of 1st Position 5
Songs in Sharp Keys 5
First Melody 5
Knoxville Dance 6
Songs in Flat Keys 7
Yankee Doodle Dandy 7
Home on the Range 8
Fingerstyle Etudes 9
Shenandoah 9
Amazing Grace 9
Piece in F Major 10
Prelude in G Minor 11
Ride the C Train 12
Time Test 1 13
Guitar Legends: Jimmy Page 14

Unit 2: Introduction to the Notes in 2nd
and 3rd Position 15
Introduction to Major Scales in 2nd and 3rd Position ... 16
Etudes in Sharp Keys 18
Fingerstyle Pieces in 2nd and 3rd Position 20
Blues in the Beginning 20
Etude in G 21
Major and Minor Triads in 2nd and 3rd Position 22
Walking by the Beach 23
Groovin' in D Minor 23
Time Test 2 24
Guitar Legends: Tommy Emmanuel 25

Unit 3: Blues in A—Switching Positions 26
The Blues Form 26
Sample Blues Progressions 27
Minor Pentatonic Scale 28
Fingerstyle Blues 29
Lowdown Doggone Blues 30
Dynamics 31
Gutbucket 31
The Blues Scale 32
A Blues Scale in the Open and 2nd Positions 32
Blues Scale Licks 34
Time Test 3 35
Guitar Legends: Muddy Waters 35

Unit 4: Barre Chords—Triads 36
Major Barre-Chord Forms 36
Minor Barre-Chord Forms 37
Study Exercise 37
Major Barre Chords in a Song 38
In the Style of "Louie Louie" No. 1 38
In the Style of "Louie Louie" No. 2 38
In the Style of "Louie Louie" No. 3 39
In the Style of "Louie Louie" No. 4 39
Minor Barre Chords in a Song 40
*In the Style of
"Another Brick in the Wall (Part 2)" No. 1* 40
*In the Style of
"Another Brick in the Wall (Part 2) No. 2* 40
Switching Between Major and Minor Barre Chords
on the Same String 41
In the Style of "All Along the Watchtower" No. 1 41
In the Style of "All Along the Watchtower" No. 2 41
Switching Between Major and Minor Barre Chords
on Different Strings 42
In the Style of "Another Brick in the Wall (Part 2)" ... 42
In the Style of "Knockin' on Heaven's Door" 43
In the Style of "I Shot the Sheriff" 43
Time Test 4 44
Guitar Legends: Charlie Christian 44

Unit 5: Power Chords 45
Introducing Power Chords 45
Songs with Power Chords 47
I Definitely Had You 47
Sounds Like Grunge 48
Nutty Bus 48
Roll You Like Sugarcane 49
Cale and Clapton 49
Alay 50
Power Chord Inversions/Slash Chords 51
Steam on the Meadow 52
Power Rockin' 53
Time Test 5 54
Guitar Legends: Ritchie Blackmore 54

Unit 6: Fingerstyle Accompaniment 55
Basic Patterns with *p, i, m, a* 55
Alternating Bass 60
Time Test 6: Fingerstyle Pattern Application 63
Poof the Giant Lizard 63
Guitar Legends: Alex De Grassi 64

Unit 7: Playing in 4th, 5th, and 6th Position 65
Major Scales in 5th Position 66
Major Scales in 4th Position 67
Etudes in Sharp Keys 68
Etudes in Flat Keys 69
Fingerstyle Etude in a Sharp Key 70
Etude in G Major 70
Fingerstyle Etude in a Flat Key 71
Etude in F Major 71
Major Triads in 5th Position 72
Minor Triads in 5th Position 73
Chord Exercise 74
Grooving in A 74
Time Test 7 75
Guitar Legends: Jeff Beck 75

Unit 8: 7th Chords 76
7th Chords as Barre Chords 77
Creek Fishin' Blues 78
Half-Note Blues 79
Doobie Do 80
Minor Funk 81

  Minor Strut 82
  Rockin' the Barre 83
 Theory Review: Chords 84
 Time Test 8 84
Guitar Legends: John McLaughlin 85

Unit 9: More Blues 86
 Blues Patterns Up the Neck 86
 Minor Blues 90
 Improvising in 5th Position 92
 A Minor Pentatonic Ideas 93
 A Blues Scale Ideas 94
 Practice Exercise 94
 Time Test 9 94
Guitar Legends: Buddy Guy 95

Unit 10: Introduction to 7th Position 96
 Scales in 7th Position 96
 Major Scales in 7th Position 97
 Melodic Etudes 99
  Harmonic Etude 1 100
  Harmonic Etude 2 101
 Major Triads in 7th and 8th Position 102
 Minor Triads in 7th and 8th Position 103
 Strumming Etudes 104
 Time Test 10 105
Guitar Legends: Ernest Ranglin 105

Unit 11: Minor Pentatonic and Blues Scales—
7th Position and Multiple-Position Fingerings 106
 Basic Fingerings in 7th Position 106
 A Minor Pentatonic Ideas 108
 A Blues Scale Ideas 109
 A Minor Pentatonic Scale Melody 110
 A Blues Scale Melody 111
 Multiple-Position A Minor Pentatonic Scale 112
 Multiple-Position A Blues Scale 113
 Multiple-Position Blues Melody 114
 Time Test 11 114
Guitar Legends: Kenny Burrell 115

Unit 12: Introduction to 9th and 10th Position 116
 Scales in 9th and 10th Position 116
 Major Scales in 9th and 10th Position 119
 Melodic Etudes 121
  Fingerstyle Etude in 9th and 10th 122
 Major and Minor Triads in 9th and 10th Position ... 123
 Strumming Etudes 124
 Time Test 12 125
Guitar Legends: Eddie Van Halen 125

Unit 13: Minor Pentatonic and Blues Scales-
9th/10th Position and Multiple-Position Fingerings 126
 Scale Fingerings in 9th/10th Position 126
 A Minor Pentatonic Scale Ideas in 9th/10th Position ... 128
 A Blues Scale Ideas in 9th/10th Position 129
 Blues Melody Using the A Minor Pentatonic Scale 130
 Blues Melody Using the A Blues Scale 131

 Multiple-Position Fingerings for A Minor Pentatonic
  and A Blues Scales 132
 Multiple-Position Blues Melody 133
 Time Test 13 134
Guitar Legends: Bonnie Raitt 134

Unit 14: Common Fingerings for Scales and Chords 135
 Major Scale 135
 Minor Pentatonic Scale 136
 Blues Scale 137
 Major Triads 137
 Minor Triads 138
 Dominant 7th Chords 139
 Minor 7th Chords 139

Chords and Songs
 Unit 15: Chords and Songs 140
  John Denver: *Take Me Home, Country Roads* 141
   Tips for Playing This Song 141
  Lou Reed: *Walk on the Wild Side* 142
   Tips for Playing This Song 142
  R.E.M.: *Losing My Religion* 143
   Tips for Playing This Song 143
  The Who: *Baba O'Riley* 144
   Tips for Playing This Song 144
  The Who: *Behind Blue Eyes* 145
   Tips for Playing This Song 145
  Green Day: *Brain Stew* 146
   Tips for Playing This Song 146
  The Rolling Stones: *Everybody Needs
  Somebody to Love* 147
   Tips for Playing This Song 147
  Green Day: *Holiday* 148
   Tips for Playing This Song 148
  The Rolling Stones: *Midnight Rambler* 149
   Tips for Playing This Song 149
  Sheryl Crow: *Soak Up the Sun* 150
   Tips for Playing This Song 150
  Eagles: *Desperado* 151
   Tips for Playing This Song 151
  Chicago: *25 or 6 to 4* 152
   Tips for Playing This Song 152

Improvisation
 Unit 16: Improvisation 153
  Improvisation Using the Major Scale 153
  Exercises 154
  Improvisation Using the Minor Pentatonic Scale 155
  Combining the Major Scale and
   Minor Pentatonic Scale in Improvisation 157

Time Test Answers 158

Common Fingerings 160

Foreword

GUITAR 101, BOOK 2

In *Guitar 101,* Book 2, we continue our journey into guitar performance. To get the most out of this text, the student should have a comprehensive understanding of the concepts and competency for the skills covered in *Guitar 101,* Book 1. The goal of this course is to learn notes, chords, and scales up the neck of the guitar through the 12th position, while incorporating this knowledge by performing songs in a variety of styles. Upon completion of this text, students will be able to play across the length of the guitar fretboard in a variety of genres and settings. Students will learn to read music, play chords, and improvise from the 1st to the 12th position.

Like the first book, *Guitar 101,* Book 2 is presented in three sections. This text works in tandem with *Guitar 101, Pop* (44143), the companion repertoire book of popular songs. Book 2 is divided into three sections that are designed to be flexible enough to be introduced concurrently at the discretion of the teacher.

Technique and Reading Music

In this section, students continue their study of standard music notation and tablature (TAB), while becoming conversant with the notes across the neck of the guitar. In learning this material, students will understand how certain fingerings and patterns relate to one another as we move up the neck. This will allow for greater connection to the fretboard, as well as a methodology for organizing notes, chords, and patterns on the guitar. At the same time, students will engage with this material in a very musical fashion. All concepts will be presented using real musical examples that allow for greater engagement, providing practical experience for the student.

Chords and Songs

In this section, students will be exposed to the key components of 12 classic popular songs. These songs are common for guitarists to learn and come from a variety of styles. Additionally, they can be integrated with various chapters of the Technique and Reading Music section, for an enhanced musical and learning experience.

Improvisation

This section ties together the scales, chords, and styles covered throughout the text, and presents the material in a way that can be applied to improvisational performance. Here, students will build upon their improvisation experience from Book 1 and start moving around the neck of the guitar. Students will learn to approach improvisation from a variety of perspectives, including diatonic improvisation and approaching the same progression using multiple methods.

Acknowledgements

Many thanks to Nat Gunod and Martha Masters for their input, patience, and guidance with this text. Also, I am grateful for each and every guitar student I have had the honor to work with—this text is the result of those relationships. I would especially like to acknowledge the faculty and students of LaGuardia Community College. Your work and presence inspires me daily.

Technique and Reading Music

UNIT 1: REVIEW OF 1ST POSITION

OBJECTIVES

Upon completion of this unit, the student will:

- Be able to read and perform single-note *(monophonic)* melodies in open position and 1st position, in multiple keys
- Be able to read and perform fingerstyle pieces that include accompaniment or concurrent voices or parts *(polyphonic)* in open position and 1st position, and in multiple keys

The following examples are considered to be in open position and 1st position, because, in both, the 1st finger is located at the 1st fret. These examples will refresh your knowledge of playing in key signatures.

SONGS IN SHARP KEYS

Example 1.1 is in the key of G Major and 1.2 is in the key of E Major. Pay close attention to the accidentals in each. In Example 1.1, notice the *1st* and *2nd endings* (second and third measure of the fourth system). These tell you to play from the beginning of the piece through to the 1st ending, and when you get to the repeat sign, go back and play from the beginning, skip over the 1st ending, and play from the 2nd ending to the end of the piece.

First Melody

1.1

Unit 1   Technique and Reading Music   5

Knoxville Dance

1.2

Songs in Flat Keys

Example 1.3 is in the key of F Major, and 1.4 is in the key of E♭ Major. Pay close attention to the accidentals in each.

Yankee Doodle Dandy

1.3

Home on the Range

1.4

FINGERSTYLE ETUDES

Following are fingerstyle etudes in 1st position. These examples will reinforce your skill for playing in 1st position, while also teaching you some important repertoire.

Below is an arrangement of the classic hymn "Amazing Grace."

* This indictates that you should barre your 1st finger across all six strings at the first fret.
  (The Roman numeral indicates the fret and the subscript Arabic numeral tells how many strings to barre.)

Following is a solo guitar piece in F Major. Note there are two sets of 1st and 2nd endings. Play through the 1st ending, then go back to the beginning or previous repeat sign and play, skipping over the 1st ending and finishing with the 2nd ending.

Piece in F Major

(From the Anna Magdalena Bach Notebook)

1.7

The following is an original composition in G Minor.

Prelude in G Minor

Tom Dempsey

1.8

This next song is in the style of "Take the A Train," composed by Billy Strayhorn and made famous by Duke Ellington. Though written in the key of C, it includes many different accidentals. You can play this song fingerstyle or with a pick. In addition, this tune has a swing feel. This concept was introduced briefly on page 124 of Guitar 101, Book 1. It means that eighth notes are not played evenly, but rather as a triplet divided into a quarter note and an eighth note.

This:
Swing Eighths

Should be played like:

Ride the C Train

1.9

Swing Eighths

Time Test 1

In the following examples, identify the name of each note, the string and fret where each note is played, and the rhythm of the notes. Write the name of each note and the rhythm of the line above the staff. Identify where each note is played and with what finger under the staff. Checkout the example below.

Example

No. 1

No. 2

Guitar Legends: Jimmy Page

Profile
- Began career as a studio musician in London, England
- Was a member of The Yardbirds from 1966–1968
- Founded Led Zeppelin in 1968
- One of the most influential rock guitarists in history
- Together with singer Robert Plant and bassist John Paul Jones, Page received the Kennedy Center Honor Award for Led Zeppelin's contributions to American culture through the performing arts

Style
- Heavily influenced by acoustic folk music and blues
- Known for huge-sounding riffs and some of the most influential rock guitar solos in history
- Played acoustic guitar parts in alternate tunings to create ambient soundscapes

Suggested Listening
- "Rock and Roll"
- "Good Times Bad Times"
- "Heartbreaker"
- "Stairway to Heaven"

UNIT 2: INTRODUCTION TO THE NOTES IN 2ND AND 3RD POSITION

OBJECTIVES

Upon completion of this unit, the student will:

- Be able to perform single-note melodies in 2nd and 3rd positions in multiple keys
- Be able to perform fingerstyle pieces in 2nd and 3rd positions in multiple keys
- Know how to play major scales in 2nd and 3rd positions
- Know how to play major and minor triads in 2nd and 3rd positions

Let's move into 2nd position, where the left-hand 1st finger is located at the 2nd fret. We'll start with a C Major scale.

2.1

Below is an example of all the natural notes in 2nd position.

2.2

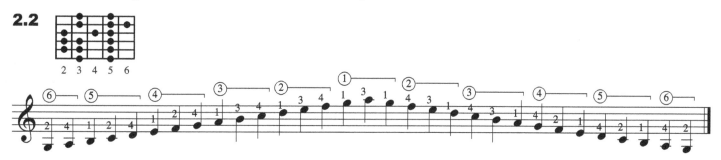

Following is an example of all the chromatic notes in 2nd position. In this example, the non-natural notes are indicated with sharps. Note that the pinky is stretching to the 6th fret. In any given position, we can momentarily stretch one fret lower or higher and then return to the standard position.

2.3

* ⑤———— This a string indication. Play all notes under this line on the string indicated.

Introduction to Major Scales in 2nd and 3rd Position

Following are scale fingerings to practice in 2nd and 3rd positions. These examples will give you a better grasp of the notes in these positions and will help you gain a better understanding of the fretboard.

2.4—C Major Scale

2.5—D Major Scale

2.6—G Major Scale

2.7—A Major Scale

2.8—B♭ Major Scale

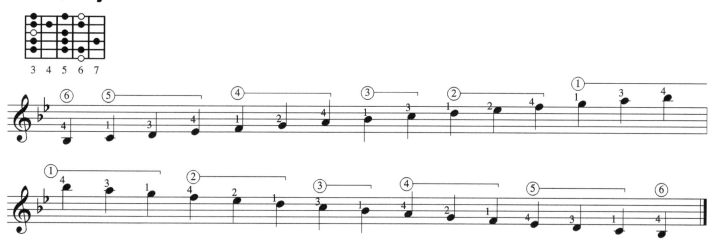

2.9—E Major Scale

2.10—F Major Scale

ETUDES IN SHARP KEYS

Below are etudes in various keys introduced in the scales above. The fingering that was used in those scales should also be applied to these etudes.

2.11—Etude in C Major

2.12—Etude in D Major

2.13—Etude in G Major

2.14—Etude in A Major

2.15—Etude in E Major

2.16—Etude in F Major

2.17—Etude in B♭ Major

Fingerstyle Pieces in 2nd and 3rd Position

While "Blues in the Beginning" is in the key of G Major, there are a number of accidentals required to create the chords found in a typical 12-bar blues chord progression. (For more on the blues, see page 26 of this book.)

Blues in the Beginning

2.18

Below is a fingerstyle etude in the key of G Major.

Etude in G

2.19

Major and Minor Triads in 2nd and 3rd Position

To better familiarize you with the notes in 2nd and 3rd position, we'll look now at chords located in these positions. When learning these chords, try to identify the various scale degrees used to construct them. Also, note that because these forms do not use open strings, they are moveable, so they will be placed in other keys as we move up the guitar neck.

2.20

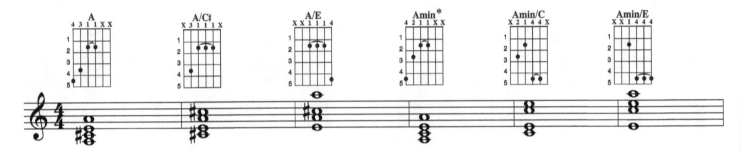

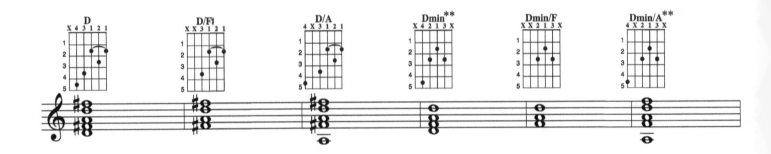

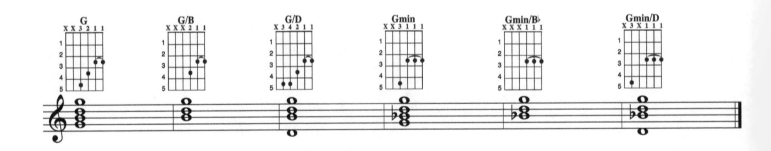

* Minor chord symbols are often abbreviated as "min" or "m."

** These voicings might be a little difficult. Do not spend too much time with them if they cause discomfort. Always stop and take a break if you experience pain while you practice.

Following are two etudes that use many of the chords introduced on the previous page.

Time Test 2

Identify the following notes and where they are played in the 2nd and 3rd positions.

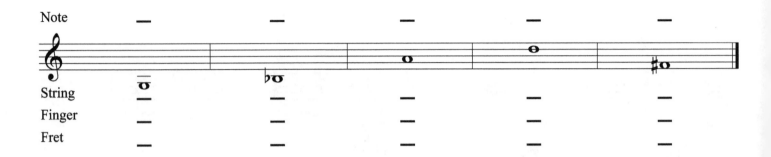

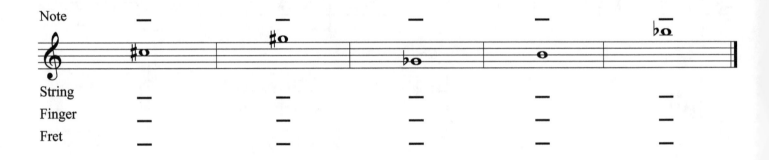

Guitar Legends: Tommy Emmanuel

Profile
- Born in New South Wales, Australia
- Influenced by the musical style of Chet Atkins
- Has performed with Chet Atkins, Eric Clapton, George Martin, John Denver, and many others
- One of the most influential acoustic solo guitarists on the scene today

Style
- Heavily influenced by acoustic folk music and blues
- Known for solo guitar arrangements that utilize Travis picking and other sophisticated elements of solo guitar performance
- Uses alternate tunings to create ambient soundscapes
- Plays using a combination of thumb pick and fingers

Suggested Listening
- "Classical Gas"
- "Lewis & Clark"
- "Guitar Boogie"
- "Angelina"

UNIT 3: BLUES IN A—SWITCHING POSITIONS

OBJECTIVES

Upon completion of this unit, the student will:

- Be able to perform blues progressions in different positions
- Be able to play the A Minor Pentatonic scale and related licks in multiple positions
- Be able to play the A Blues scale and related licks in multiple positions
- Begin to improvise using the A Minor Pentatonic scale and A Blues scale

THE BLUES FORM

The blues is one of the most influential genres in modern popular music. The classic blues form is a 12-bar progression (*12-bar blues*), as shown below. This progression is in the key of A (as are all the progressions in this unit)—however, the blues progression can be played in any key. In the example below, notice that Roman numerals I (one), IV (four), and V (five) are indicated for each chord. These Roman numerals represent chords built on the 1st, 4th, and 5th degrees of the major scale; in this case, the A Major scale (A is the 1st degree, D is the 4th degree, and E is the 5th). While there are many variations to the blues form, the basic form below can be considered the *classic blues progression*. (For more on Roman numerals and diatonic harmony, see page 153.)

3.1—Classic 12-Bar Blues Progression

Sample Blues Progressions

Below is a basic blues progression that utilizes *power chords* (two-note chords made up of a root and a 5th; for more on power chords, see page 45). You can play the eighth-note rhythm with a straight (rock) or swing (jazz or shuffle) feel.

3.2—Blues Progression 1

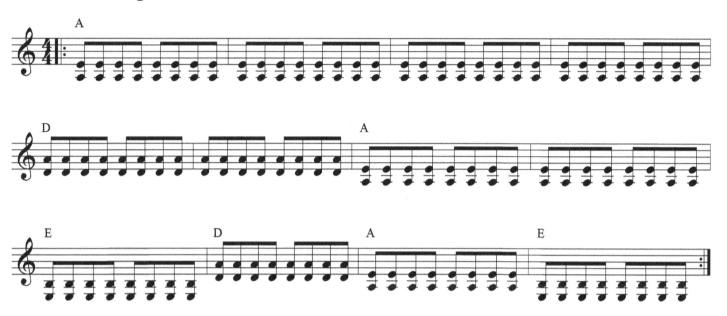

Next is a variation on Blues Progression 1. For each chord, we alternate between two different notes (the 5th and 6th) to give it a *boogie-woogie* type of sound. This helps to create more momentum. Boogie-woogie is a common blues feel that became popular in the 1920s.

3.3—Blues Progression 2

3.4—Blues Progression 3

The next progression is another variation on the classic boogie-woogie sound. It features a pattern that alternates between three different notes— the 5th, 6th, and ♭7th—on each chord. (Note: When a flat sign appears before a scale degree, that note is just lowered by one half step.)

Minor Pentatonic Scale

The *minor pentatonic scale* is an important sound associated with the blues. It is a five-note scale that can be used to create solo and melody ideas over a chord progression, and it consists of scale degrees 1–♭3–4–5–♭7. Below is the A Minor Pentatonic scale in open position, first shown in a one-octave form and then with all of its notes in open position. As shown below, practice this scale by always returning to its *tonic*, or root, A. This will help you get the sound of the scale in your ears as well as under your fingers. TAB is included to help you learn these scales and the licks that follow.

3.5—A Minor Pentatonic Scale

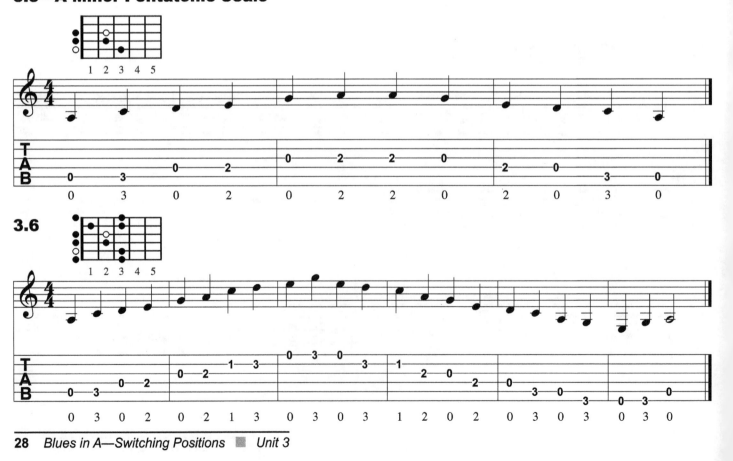

FINGERSTYLE BLUES

Licks are musical phrases that can be learned and used in your playing, and they can also serve as springboards for your own ideas. Every musician learns licks at one point or another, as they provide great examples of how scales can be applied in a musical fashion. Below are four licks based on the A Minor Pentatonic scale. Learn these licks and begin to apply them when improvising.

3.7—A Minor Pentatonic Lick 1

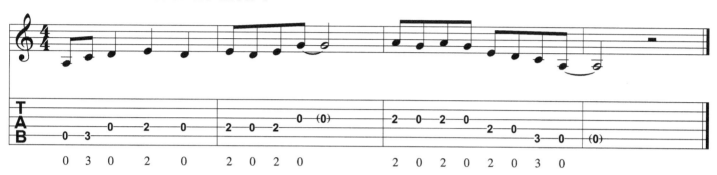

3.8—A Minor Pentatonic Lick 2

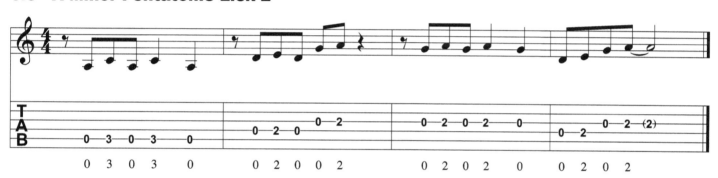

3.9—A Minor Pentatonic Lick 3

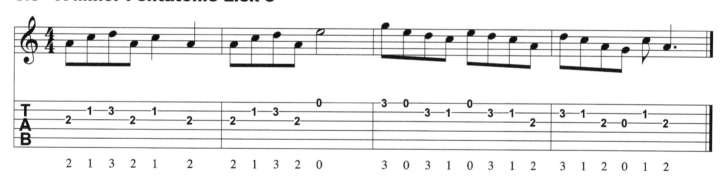

3.10—A Minor Pentatonic Lick 4

Next, we have a couple of fingerstyle 12-bar blues pieces. Both can be played using straight eighths or with more of a swing feel. Each way will produce a unique-sounding arrangement.

Lowdown Doggone Blues

3.11

DYNAMICS

The next example is similar to the previous piece but features the A Minor Pentatonic scale. Note the *hand mute* technique, indicated with an "X" note head (×). To execute a hand mute, slap the fingers of your right hand against the strings to create a percussive sound. Try playing this piece using both a straight feel and a swing feel.

Gutbucket

3.12

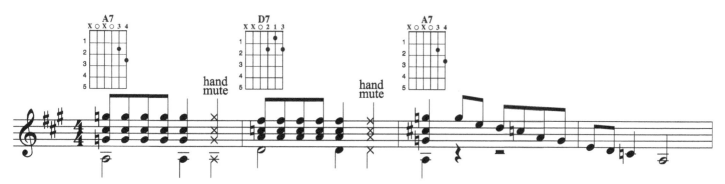

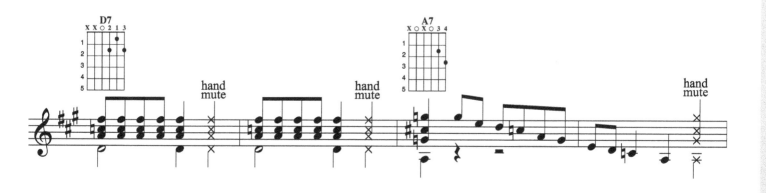

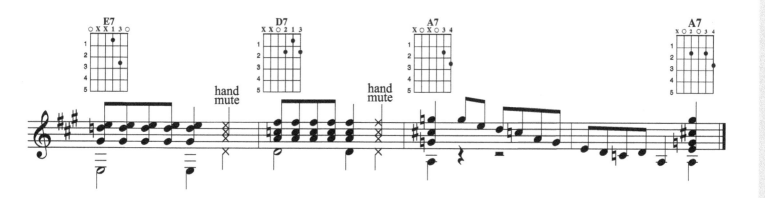

The Blues Scale

Now, let's look at another characteristic sound of the blues, the *blues scale*. The blues scale is the same as the minor pentatonic scale except it includes one additional note, the ♭5. This is a *blue note*, because of its bluesy sound. (Other blue notes are the ♭3 and ♭7 when applied over a major chord or dominant 7th chord.)

Below is a comparison between the A Minor Pentatonic and A Blues scales. Through the presence of the ♭5, notice that the blues scale has a sound and identity all its own.

3.13
A Minor Pentatonic Scale

A Blues Scale

A Blues Scale in the Open and 2nd Positions

The next four examples are fingerings for the A Blues scale in the open and 2nd positions. There are two versions for each position—practice them both. The first is a one-octave fingering that allows you to get the sound of the scale in your ears. The second features all the notes in that position and eventually resolves back to the tonic; this version will help your ear recognize the sound of the scale by orienting it to where the tonic is located.

Because you are now familiar with the open and 2nd positions, the following examples do not include TAB.

3.14—Blues Scale in Open Position

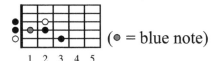
(● = blue note)

3.15

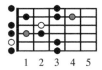

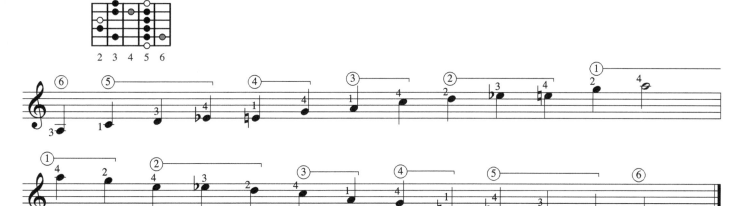

3.16—Blues Scale in 2nd Position

3.17

BLUES SCALE LICKS

Below are some blues scale licks for you to practice and learn. These examples use the two fingerings covered on the previous page. Learn the licks exactly as written, and then try to develop licks of your own using these examples as starting points.

Blues Scale Licks in Open Position

3.18—Open Position Lick 1

3.19—Open Position Lick 2

3.20—Open Position Lick 3

3.21—Open Position Lick 4

Blues Scale Licks in 2nd Position

3.22—2nd Position Lick 1

3.23—2nd Position Lick 2

3.24—2nd Position Lick 3

3.25—2nd Position Lick 4

Time Test 3

From memory, write out the notes of the A Minor Pentatonic scale and A Blues scale below.

A Minor Pentatonic Scale

A Blues Scale

Guitar Legends: Muddy Waters

Profile
- Born in Issaquena County, Mississippi
- Influenced by the musical styles of Robert Johnson, Blind Lemon Jefferson, Lonnie Johnson, and Son House
- Has influenced important rock guitarists, including Eric Clapton, Keith Richards, Angus Young, and Jimmy Page
- Well-known as a singer, songwriter, harmonica player, and guitarist

Style
- Heavily influenced by Delta blues music from Mississippi
- One of the key originators of the Chicago blues sound
- Master of playing bottleneck slide guitar
- One of the first blues guitarists to play the electric guitar
- Applied the sound and style of Delta blues to the electric guitar

Suggested Listening
- "Rollin' Stone"
- "Hoochie Coochie Man"
- "Got My Mojo Workin'"
- "Mannish Boy"

UNIT 4: BARRE CHORDS—TRIADS

OBJECTIVES

Upon completion of this unit, the student will:

- Know how to play major barre chords with roots on the 6th and 5th strings
- Know how to play minor barre chords with roots on the 6th and 5th strings
- Be able to switch between chords with roots on the 6th and 5th strings
- Be able to play songs using barre chords

In *Guitar 101,* Book 1 we introduced barre chords and played them in various tunes. In this unit, we will review our triad barre-chord forms and use them in more sample tunes.

MAJOR BARRE-CHORD FORMS

In Example 4.1, G is a 6th-string barre-chord form and C (both versions) is a 5th-string barre-chord form. All three of these major chords are triads because they are made up of only three notes, even though some of those notes are repeated.

4.1

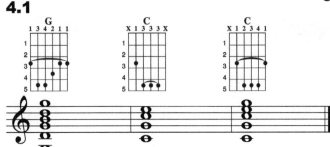

As you can see to the left, the G chord consists of the following notes: G–D–G–B–D–G. While there are six notes being played, there are actually only three different notes: G–B–D. The notes G–B–D make up a G Major triad. A similar situation is present in both versions of the C barre chord. In the first example, there are four notes: C–G–C–E. However, only three of these notes are different, C–E–G, the notes of the C Major triad. The second version of the C chord consists of five notes: C–G–C–E–G. Once again, there are actually only three different notes here, C–E–G, the notes of a C Major triad. The particular arrangement of notes within a chord is called a *voicing*. So, the different versions of C are different voicings of the same chord.

4.2

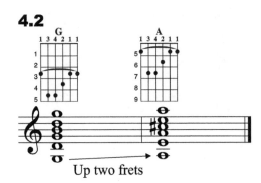

Up two frets

As discussed in Book 1 and mentioned above, there are two basic types of barre-chord forms, the 6th-string form (with the root on the 6th string) and the 5th-string form (with the root on the 5th string). These forms are moveable, which means you can move them anywhere on the neck and still have a major barre chord. For instance, the G chord above is a 6th-string barre-chord form, which means the root is on the 6th string. In this case, the note on the 6th string, 3rd fret is G. If we move the form up a whole step so that the note on the 6th string is A, we now have an A Major barre chord (see Example 4.2.

Let's look briefly at the two C chords in Example 4.1. In the first voicing, which is commonly used in rock and pop music, we play the root with our 1st finger. We play the other notes by placing the

3rd finger across the 4th, 3rd, and 2nd strings. The 1st string is muted by the bottom of the 3rd finger. At first, this voicing can be a bit tricky, but after some practice, it can be a very effective.

For an alternate voicing of the A chord, the 1st finger barres strings 1–5. The notes that were played with the 3rd finger in the first voicing are now played with the 2nd, 3rd, and 4th fingers. This voicing is commonly found in classical and folk music. Both of these voicings are important to learn.

Minor Barre-Chord Forms

4.3

Now, let's look at our minor barre-chord forms. The G Minor chord is a 6th-string barre chord form and the C Minor chord is a 5th-string barre chord form.

The G Minor chord consists of the notes G–D–G–B♭–D–G. While we are playing six strings here, there are only three different notes, G–B♭–D, the notes of a G Minor triad.

The C Minor chord is made up of the notes C–G–C–E♭–G; of these notes, only three of them are different, C–E♭–G, the notes of a C Minor triad.

Both of the forms above are moveable, which means you can move them anywhere on the neck and still have a minor barre chord. For instance, the C Minor chord above is a 5th-string barre-chord form, which means the root is on the 5th string. In this case, the note on the 5th string, 3rd fret is C. If we move the form up a whole step so that the note on the 5th string is D, we now have a D Minor barre chord.

Study Exercise

Move each of the major and minor barre chords covered above from 3rd position to 1st position. Play each chord and then identify it by saying its name aloud. From 1st position, move the chords up one fret at a time, identifying each as you ascend. As you ascend, identify the chords with non-natural roots as sharps (for instance, a 6th-string root at the 2nd fret would be F♯). As you descend, identify the chords with non-natural roots as flats (a 6th-string root at the 2nd fret would be G♭). This process will help you play these chords more effectively while strengthening your knowledge of the fretboard.

MAJOR BARRE CHORDS IN A SONG

The next four examples are in the style of the song "Louie Louie." This tune was written by Richard Berry and made famous by the Kingsmen. Each example utilizes a different set of barre chords to familiarize you with these forms. We begin by sticking to one form, and on the following page, we start mixing forms. Practice these examples slowly and accurately. Make sure all the strings are ringing out clearly.

In the Style of "Louie Louie" No. 1

(6th-String Barre-Chord Forms)

4.4

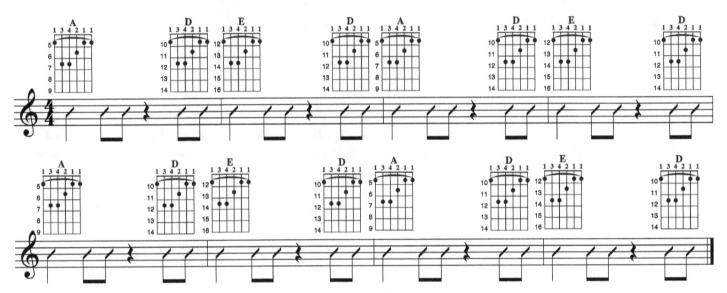

In the Style of "Louie Louie" No. 2

(5th-String Barre-Chord Forms)

4.5

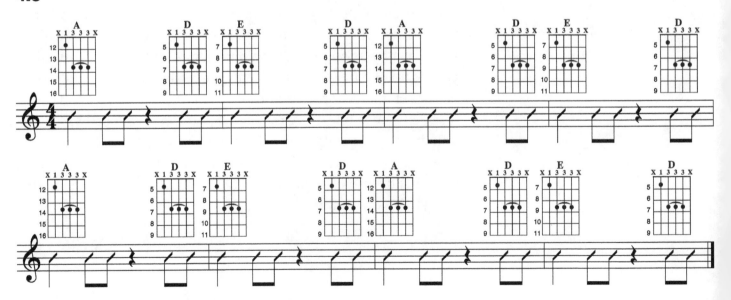

38 Barre Chords—Triads ■ Unit 4

In the Style of "Louie Louie" No. 3

(Alternating 5th- and 6th-String Forms)

4.6

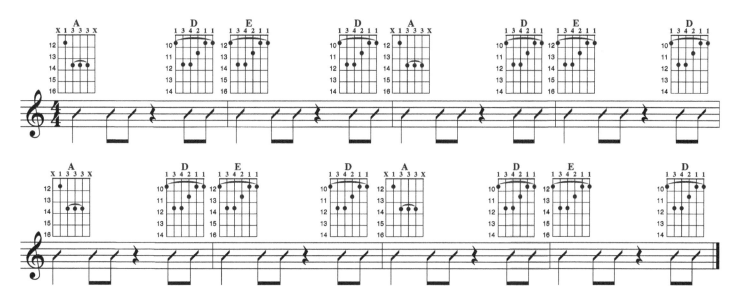

In the Style of "Louie Louie" No. 4

(Alternating 6th- and 5th-String Forms)

4.7

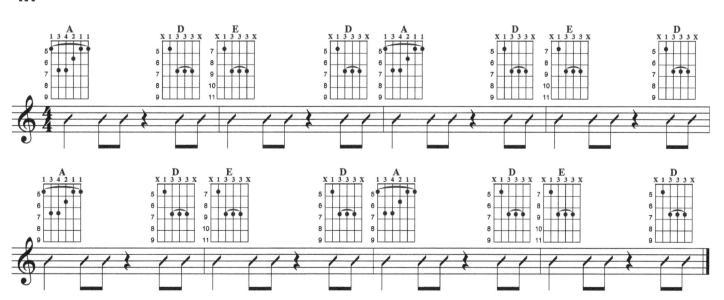

Minor Barre Chords in a Song

The next two examples are in the style of Pink Floyd's "Another Brick in the Wall (Part 2)." Example 4.8 features the 6th-string minor barre-chord form and Example 4.9 features the 5th-string minor barre-chord form.

In the Style of "Another Brick in the Wall (Part 2)" No. 1

(6th-String Barre-Chord Form)

4.8

In the Style of "Another Brick in the Wall (Part 2)" No. 2

(5th-String Barre-Chord Form)

4.9

Switching Between Major and Minor Barre Chords on the Same String

Below are two examples in the style of the song "All Along the Watchtower." The tune was written by Bob Dylan but recorded by many different artists (including Jimi Hendrix) and in different keys. Example 4.10 is in the key of A Minor, and Example 4.11 is in the key of B Minor. The two versions will help you become accustomed to switching between major and minor barre chords on a single string. Practice these songs slowly and accurately.

In the Style of "All Along the Watchtower" No. 1

(5th-String Barre-Chord Forms)

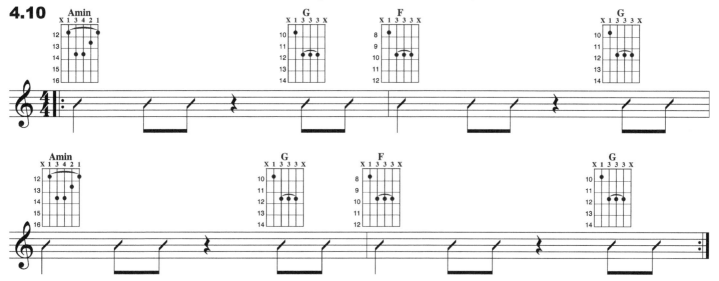

In the Style of "All Along the Watchtower" No. 2

(6th-String Barre-Chord Forms)

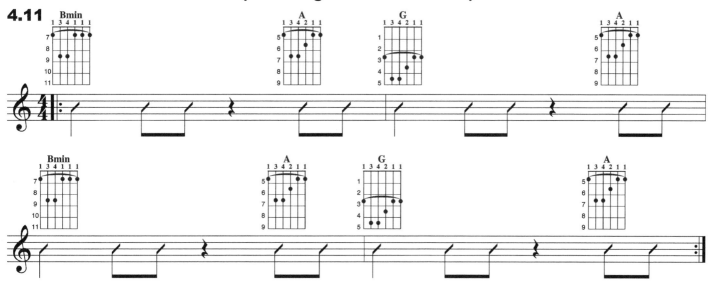

SWITCHING BETWEEN MAJOR AND MINOR BARRE CHORDS ON DIFFERENT STRINGS

The next examples are songs that switch between major and minor barre-chord forms with roots on the 5th and 6th strings. These songs bring together many of the skills covered in this unit. As always, practice them slowly and accurately at first, and then build up speed.

In the Style of "Another Brick in the Wall (Part 2)"

4.12

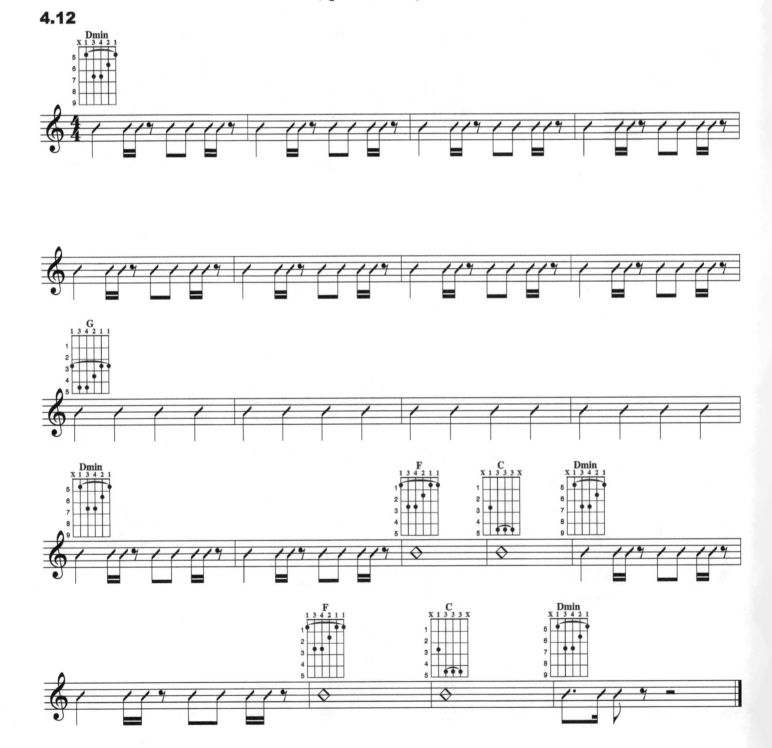

In the Style of "Knockin' on Heaven's Door"

4.13

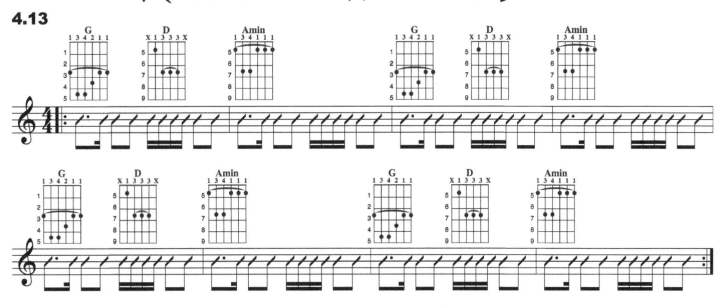

In the Style of "I Shot the Sheriff"

4.14

Time Test 4

Identify the following barre chords with the appropriate chord name.

Guitar Legends: Charlie Christian

Profile
- Born in Bonham, Texas but moved at a young age to Oklahoma City, Oklahoma
- Influenced by the musical styles of horn players Lester Young and Herschel Evans
- Has influenced many important jazz guitarists, including Wes Montgomery, Kenny Burrell, George Benson, and Jim Hall
- The first guitarist to play a recorded jazz solo on the electric guitar

Style
- Played long arpeggiated melodies that were influenced by the riff-based soloing techniques of horn players
- Performed with Benny Goodman's band where he gained national acclaim
- Was in the house band at Minton's Playhouse in Harlem, New York, where he played nightly with musicians like Dizzy Gillespie, Charlie Parker, Thelonious Monk, and Don Byas
- Was one of the major influences on the sound of bebop

Suggested Listening
- "Solo Flight"
- "Rose Room"
- "Grand Slam"
- "Airmail Special"

UNIT 5: POWER CHORDS

OBJECTIVES

Upon completion of this unit, the student will:

- Be able to play power chords with roots on the 6th and 5th strings
- Be able to play inverted power chords
- Apply power chords to songs

INTRODUCING POWER CHORDS

In Unit 4, we looked at triads voiced as barre chords. We learned how to play both major and minor barre chords and applied them to songs. In rock and pop music, there is a different kind of chord that evolved out of the barre-chord sound, and it is known as the *power chord*. Power chords have their historic roots in the blues of the 1950s, specifically, from Sun Records recordings by guitarists Willie Johnson and Pat Hare. Later, the sound of power chords infiltrated rock music through the playing of guitarists Pete Townshend, Jimmy Page, and many others. The person first credited with using power chords in rock music was a little-known guitarist named Link Wray.

Power chords consist of two chord tones: the root and the 5th. The 3rd of the chord is omitted in these voicings, which allows for a much more open-sounding chord that is neither major nor minor. However, the way power chords function within a progression leads the listener to either a major or minor sound. The chord symbol for a power chord consists of the root name followed by the number "5," so for instance: A5, D5, E♭5, etc.

For our purposes, we are going to focus on two different types of power chords. Like the barre chords from the previous unit, each type has a 6th-string form and a 5th-string form. Also like barre chords, these power chords are moveable. The first type of power chord we'll look at is a two-string voicing. These power chords are both in *root position*, meaning the root of the chord is the lowest note sounded.

5.1

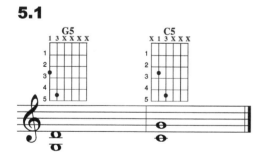

Remember, both of the shapes above are moveable, so we can move them to any location on the fretboard and still have a power chord. For instance, move G5 up two frets and we'll have A5; move C5 up two frets and we'll have D5.

Unit 5 ■ Power Chords 45

The second type of power chord we'll look at is a three-string voicing, which is made up of the root, 5th, and octave of the root. Because of the additional note, this power chord has a thicker sound than the two-string voicing.

5.2

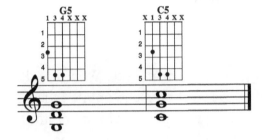

Try practicing these chords with the exercises below.

5.3

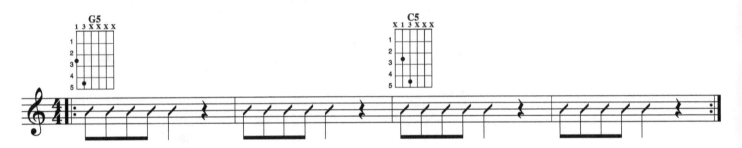

5.4

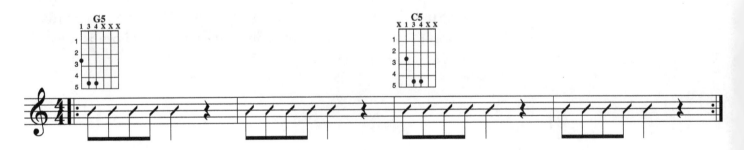

46 Power Chords ■ Unit 5

Songs with Power Chords

The next song is in the style of "You Really Got Me" by The Kinks. This is a classic use of power chords in a rock song. You can also try using two-string voicings to play this tune.

I Definitely Had You

5.5

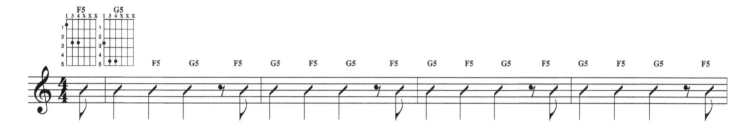

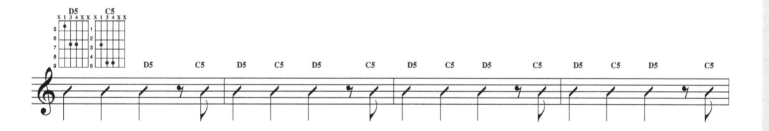

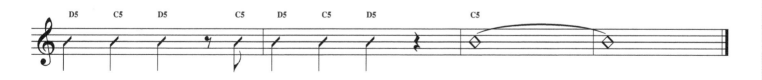

Next is a riff in the style Nirvana's "Smells Like Teen Spirit." In this example, you will be switching between 6th-string and 5th-string power chords.

Sounds Like Grunge

5.6

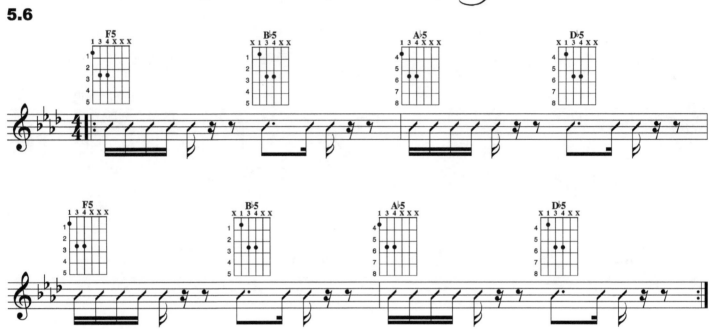

Below is an example in the style of Ozzy Osbourne's "Crazy Train." Learning this guitar part will improve your ability to move around the fretboard with power chords while integrating an open E-string power chord into the progression.

Nutty Bus

5.7

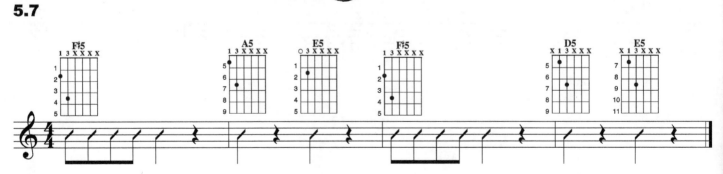

The following example is a riff in the style of The Scorpions song "Rock You Like a Hurricane." Practicing it will help you move power chords around the fretboard with greater ease.

Roll You Like Sugarcane

5.8

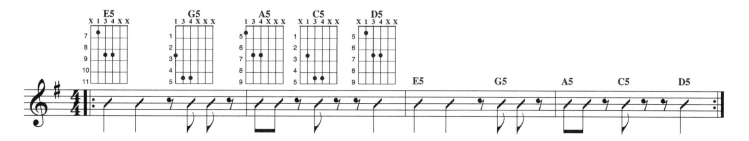

Here is a power-chord riff based on the playing of guitarists J. J. Cale and Eric Clapton.

Cale and Clapton

5.9

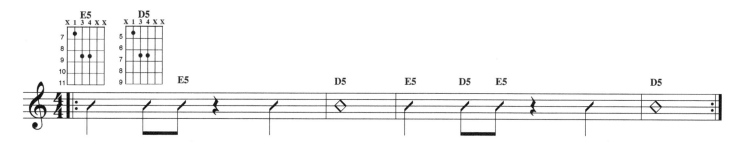

This next example is also in the style of Eric Clapton—in particular, his song "Layla." Example 5.10 has you moving power chords around the fretboard while also incorporating a single-note line. Being able to change smoothly between single notes and power chords is an important skill to learn.

Alay

5.10

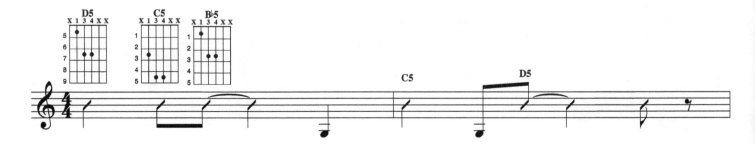

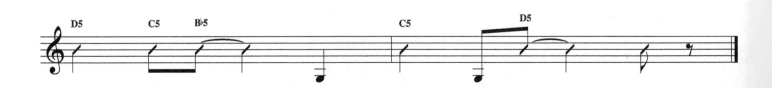

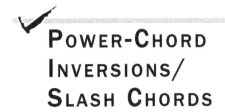

Power-Chord Inversions/ Slash Chords

In all the power chords covered so far, the root has always been the lowest note in the voicing. There are times, though, when the root will not be the lowest note—this type of chord is an *inversion*. In an inversion, the root note is placed above one or more notes in the chord; so, in the case of power chords, where there is only a root and a 5th, the 5th becomes the lowest note. Below are examples of the G5 and C5 chord voicings played as inversions. Note that chord symbols for inversions are written as *slash chords*. In a slash chord, the chord name appears to the left of the slash and the lowest note appears to the right of the slash.

5.11

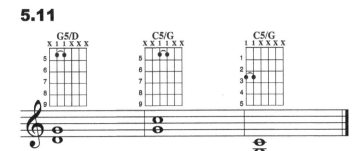

You'll notice that these chords are arguably even easier to play than the initial root-position power chords already covered. Because the notes are on adjacent strings at the same fret, you can play them with a single barred finger.

You can also intensify the sound by doubling the 5th and root an octave higher, as in the examples below.

5.12

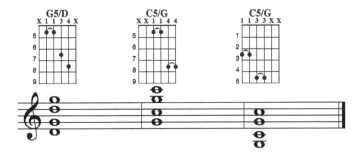

Our next example is in the style Deep Purple's classic song "Smoke on the Water," which features one of the quintessential guitar riffs of all time. This riff utilizes inverted power chords to create a thick harmonic texture. Practice this example with the pick, but also experiment by playing it fingerstyle with the thumb on the lower notes and the index finger on the upper notes—that's the way Deep Purple's guitarist, Ritchie Blackmore, played it.

Steam on the Meadow

5.13

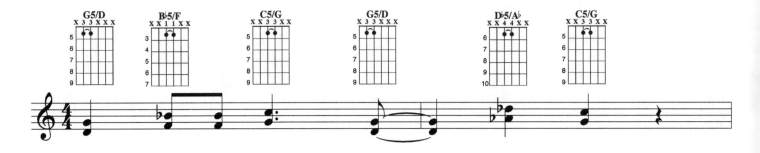

Below is a tune that utilizes inverted power chords with doubled roots and 5ths. These chords create a very thick texture, but they are a bit more challenging to move around the fretboard than the other power chords. Practice this example slowly and accurately at first, then build up speed.

Power Rockin'

5.14

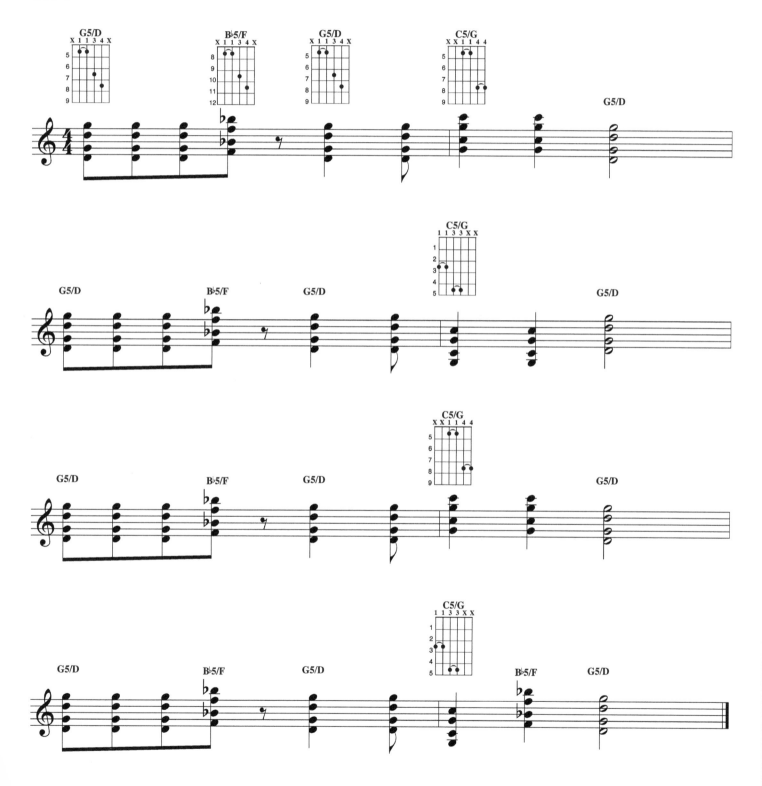

Time Test 5

Identify the following power chords.

Guitar Legends: Ritchie Blackmore

Profile
- Born in Weston-super-Mare, England
- Began his career as a studio musician and as a member of an instrumental band called The Outlaws
- Joined Deep Purple in 1968 where he made his mark as a guitarist
- Later formed the bands Rainbow and Blackmore's Night
- One of the most influential guitarists in the development of heavy metal music

Style
- Played heavily distorted guitar sounds
- Often used his thumb and index finger when soloing
- Later music often made use of the whammy bar
- Known for skillful and quick phrasing, creating memorable musical riffs and ideas in his solos

Suggested Listening
- "Smoke on the Water"
- "Child in Time"
- "Hush"
- "Black Night"

UNIT 6: FINGERSTYLE ACCOMPANIMENT

✓ OBJECTIVES

Upon completion of this unit, the student will:

- Be able to play various fingerstyle accompaniment patterns
- Be able to play various alternating-bass fingerstyle patterns
- Apply fingerstyle accompaniment patterns to songs

✓ BASIC PATTERNS WITH *p, i, m, a*

One of the skills guitarists need to learn is how to compose fingerstyle accompaniment patterns on the spot. There are many potential patterns to explore. In this unit, we will present a variety of patterns to introduce you to this style and inspire you to come up with patterns of your own.

When playing in this style, we will *arpeggiate* our chords rather than strum them. In other words, we will play the notes of the chords, predominantly, one at a time—being sure to let the notes ring out. Below is an example of how this is done with a C chord. TAB is included in the following examples to help you learn this new style.

6.1

In Example 6.1, you can see we are arpeggiating this chord in a repetitive ascending pattern. Notice the four-note pattern begins with the root of the chord and is followed by the notes G, C, and E on the 3rd, 2nd, and 1st strings. This is a simple yet common way to approach a fingerstyle accompaniment: play the root with the thumb and assign the index, middle, and ring fingers to the top three strings. Being able to do this with consistency and even phrasing is an excellent skill to acquire.

This next example takes the fingerstyle pattern we learned on the previous page and applies it to a changing chord progression. The pattern remains the same as far as right-hand finger placement. The one challenge is making sure your thumb moves to the root of the appropriate chord voicing as it changes from chord to chord. Notice how the index, middle, and ring fingers are assigned to the 3rd, 2nd, and 1st strings.

6.2

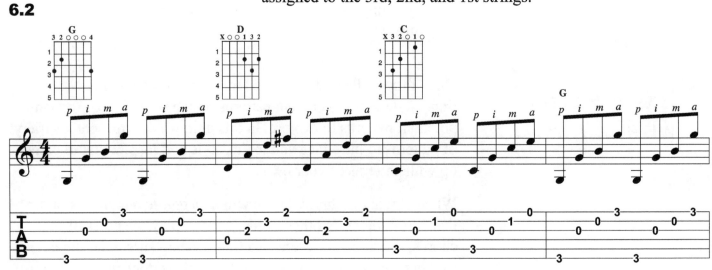

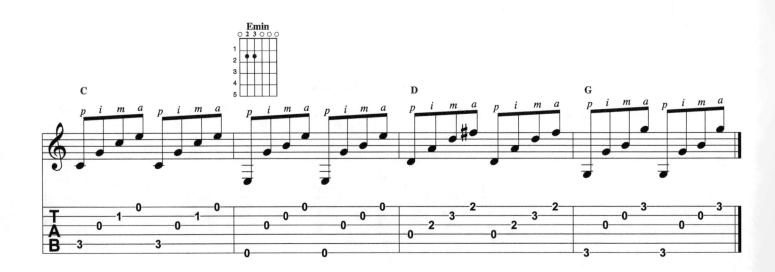

In the example below, instead of ascending the strings after the root is played, we will descend from the 1st string to the 3rd string as notated. This adds variety to your arpeggiated fingerstyle pattern. It will also accustom your fingers to learning different patterns. By mastering this and the previous pattern, you can begin to develop more independence with the right hand.

6.3

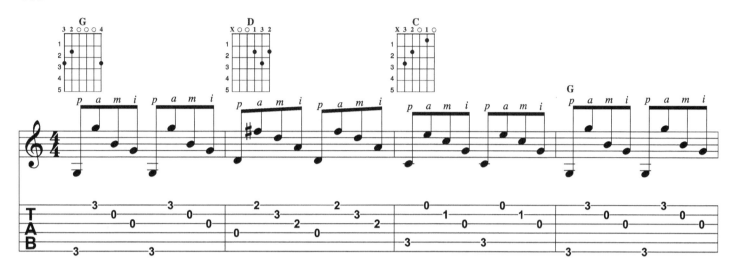

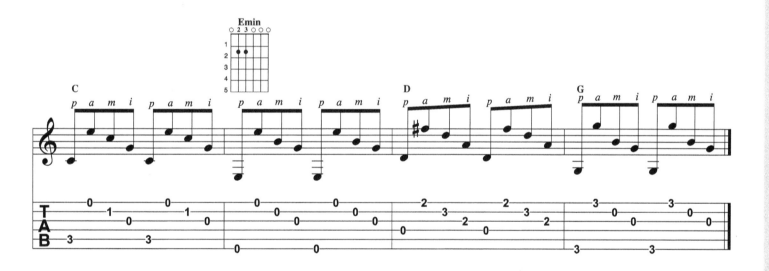

In this next pattern, we will incorporate a slightly different technique. This one engages our thumb and ring finger to play two notes simultaneously (referred to as a *pinch*) to create a sustained sound while our index and middle fingers play an *ostinato* pattern (a short pattern that repeats throughout a piece). This new technique involves some finger independence, so be sure to practice it slowly and carefully at first. Below is the basic pattern.

6.4

Now, let's apply this new pattern to the progression we used in Example 6.3.

6.5

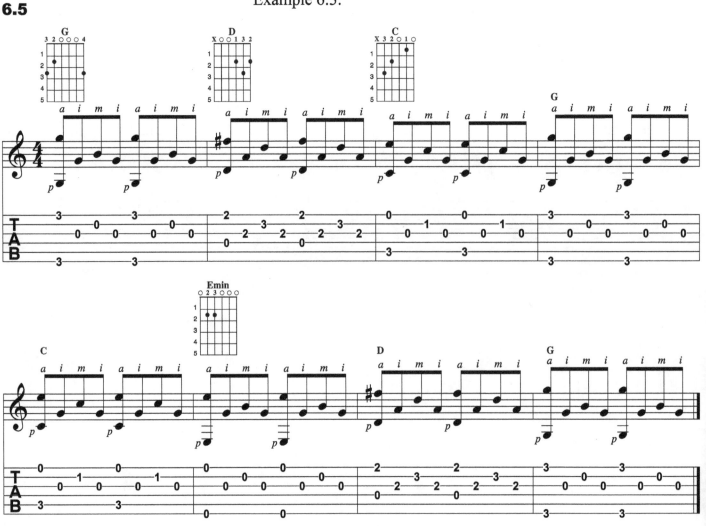

58 *Fingerstyle Accompaniment* ▪ Unit 6

The next pattern builds off of the previous one. We still have the pinch on beat 1, but the direction of the ostinato line is inverted. Additionally, we will only play the bass note on beat 1, as opposed to beats 1 and 3 like the previous pattern.

6.6

Now, let's apply the pattern to our chord progression.

6.7

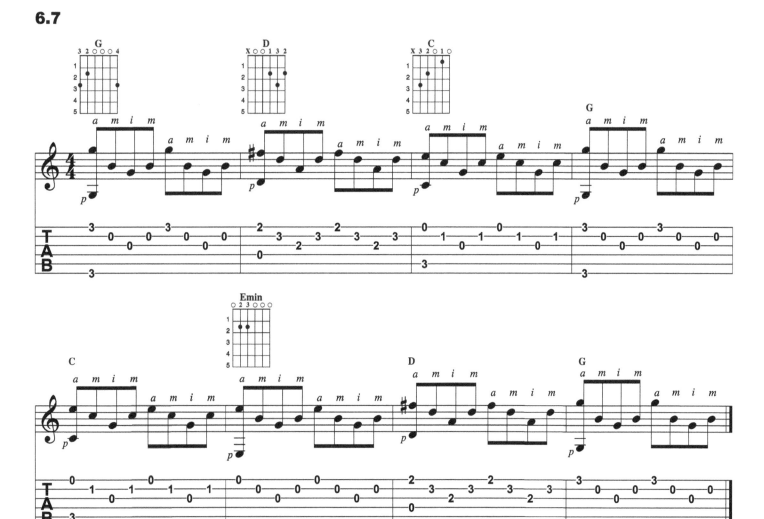

Unit 6   Fingerstyle Accompaniment   59

Alternating Bass

Another accompaniment technique that can be used to create motion is known as *alternating bass*, which works equally well when strumming with a pick or playing fingerstyle. To execute this technique, the thumb alternates between the root and another note of the chord. Sometimes, the other note is played on the string directly above the string on which the root note is played, as in the example below.

6.8

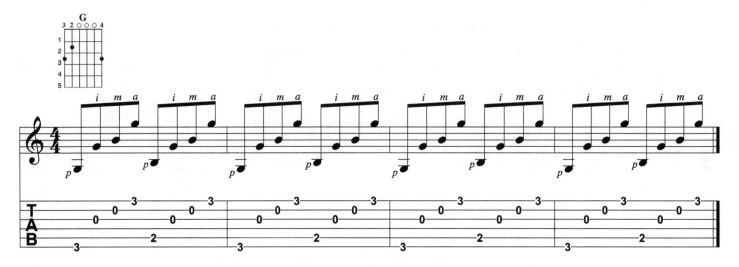

Sometimes, the root note alternates with a chord tone that is on the string directly below the string on which the root is being played.

6.9

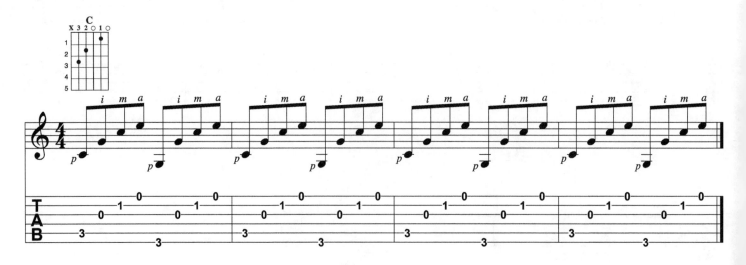

60 Fingerstyle Accompaniment   Unit 6

The following examples utilize aspects of the fingerstyle patterns covered so far, incorporating the alternating-bass technique.

6.10

Time Test 6: Fingerstyle Pattern Application

This Time Test is performance-oriented. Below is a chord progression in the style of the popular folk tune "Puff (The Magic Dragon)." As a guitarist, it is common to have music handed to you in the form below, which is called a *lead sheet*. Compose an accompaniment pattern for the song, applying the various fingerstyle patterns you learned in this chapter. You can practice by applying one pattern throughout, or combine multiple patterns or aspects of multiple patterns to the accompaniment that you develop. You are also free to develop your own patterns based on what you have learned in this chapter—but do so within 10 seconds of seeing these chords, and play without stopping.

Poof the Giant Lizard

Guitar Legends: Alex De Grassi

Profile
- Born in Yokosuka, Japan but grew up in San Francisco, California
- A self-taught guitarist
- Performed as a street musician in London after graduating from the University of California, Berkeley with a degree in economic geography
- One of the pioneering artists on the new-age record label Windham Hill

Style
- Known as a solo fingerstyle guitarist
- Incorporates alternate tunings into his compositions and arrangements
- Some of his music is influenced by music from South America

Suggested Listening
- "Turning: Turning Back"
- "Children's Dance"
- "Western"
- "The Zipper"

UNIT 7: PLAYING IN 4TH, 5TH, AND 6TH POSITION

OBJECTIVES

Upon completion of this unit, the student will:

- Be able to perform single-note melodies in 4th and 5th position in multiple keys
- Be able to perform fingerstyle pieces in 5th and 6th position in multiple keys
- Know how to play major scales in 4th and 5th position
- Know how to play major and minor triads in 4th and 5th position

In this unit, we will focus on the notes in 5th position. As we did in Unit 2, we'll look first at the C Major scale. So you can really focus on and learn the location of notes in this position, this unit will not include TAB.

7.1

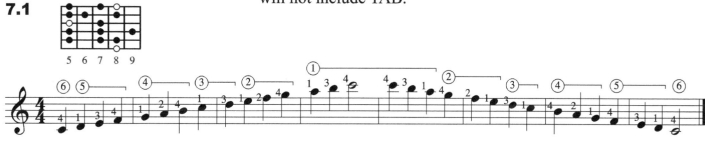

Now, let's look at all the natural notes in 5th position. Notice there are only two additional notes from the scale above: the two notes below the root on the 6th string.

7.2

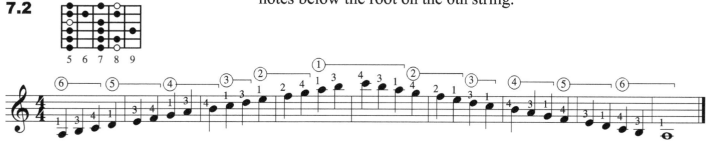

Below is an example of the notes in 5th position, including the chromatic, non-natural, notes. As we ascend, the chromatic notes are represented with sharps, and as we descend, the chromatic notes are represented with flats.

7.3

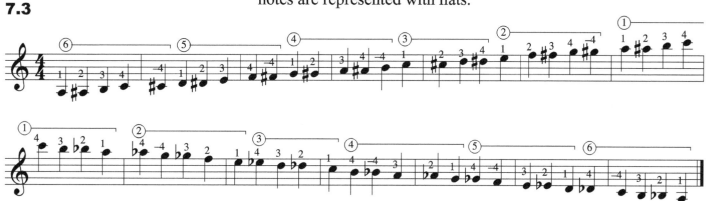

Major Scales in 5th Position

Below are major-scale fingerings in 5th position. By practicing these scales, you will learn the notes in this position as well as gain a better understanding of the fretboard. When practicing, make sure you are reading the notes and not just looking at the diagrams—this will reinforce this material and help you become a better sight-reader.

7.4—C Major Scale in 5th Position

7.5—B♭ Major Scale in 5th Position

7.6—F Major Scale in 5th Position

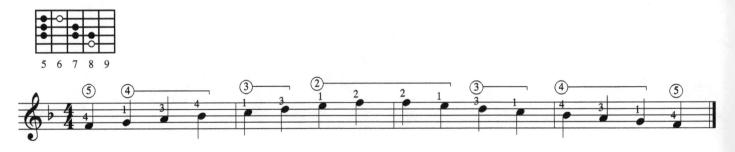

7.7—E♭ Major Scale in 5th Position

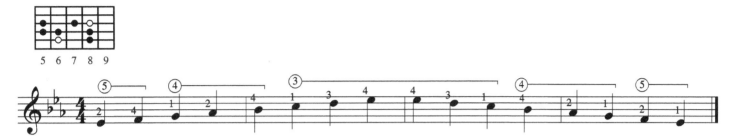

7.8—G Major Scale in 5th Position

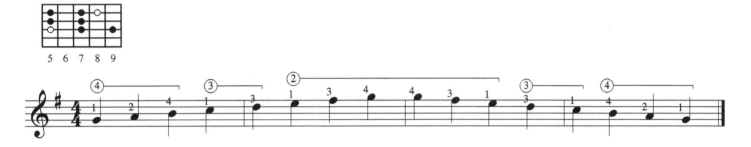

MAJOR SCALES IN 4TH POSITION

Though we are concentrating on 5th position, let's look at a couple of scales in 4th position.

7.9—A Major Scale in 4th Position

7.10—E Major Scale in 4th Position

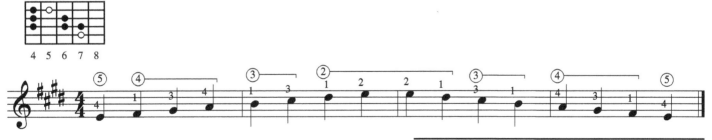

ETUDES IN SHARP KEYS

The following etudes are to be played in the 5th and 4th positions. Practice these examples using the corresponding major-scale fingerings covered in this unit. The first etude is in G Major, which lies right in 5th position; the etudes in A Major and E Major are in 4th position.

7.11—Etude in G Major

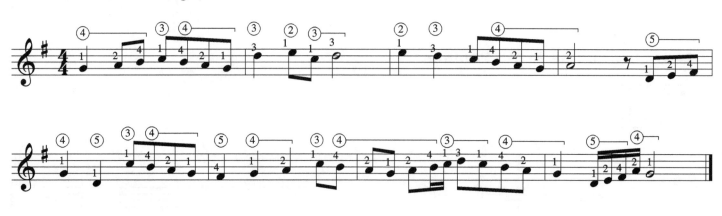

7.12—Etude in A Major

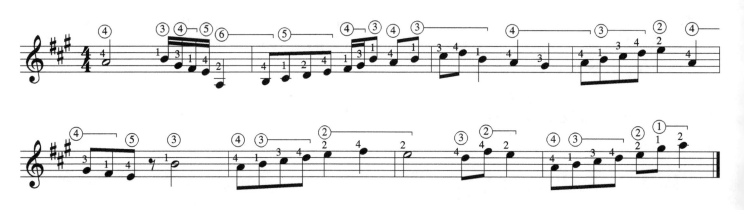

7.13—Etude in E Major

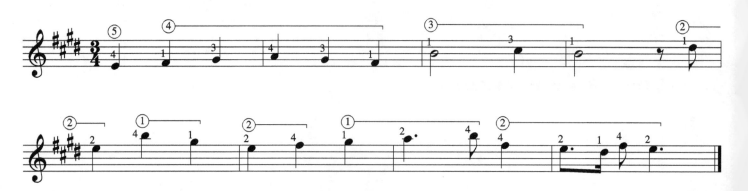

ETUDES IN FLAT KEYS

The following etudes are in flat keys and in 5th position. Learn and practice these examples using the corresponding major-scale fingerings covered in this unit.

7.14—Etude in B♭ Major

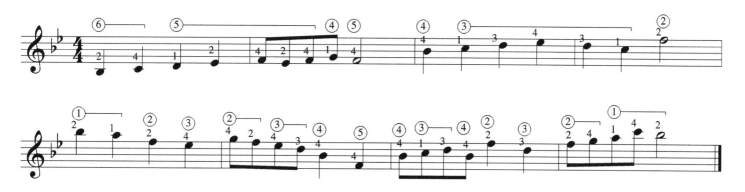

The following etude has a 6/4 time signature. This means that each quarter note gets one beat and each measure has six beats.

7.15—Etude in F Major

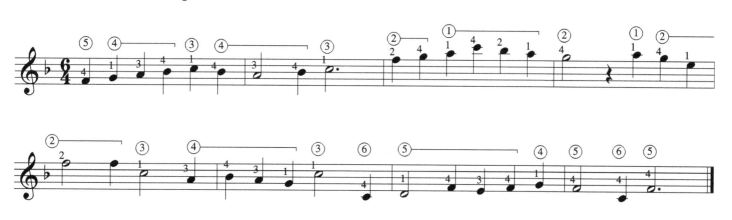

7.16—Etude in E♭ Major

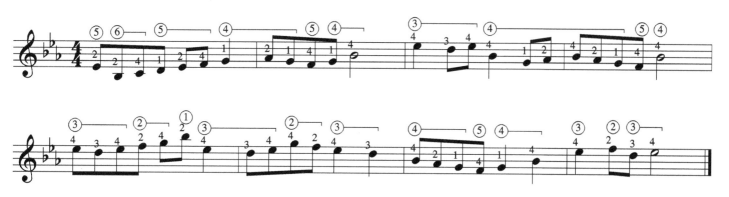

FINGERSTYLE ETUDE IN A SHARP KEY

Next is a 5th-position fingerstyle etude in the key of G Major. This example features common 5th-position chord voicings.

Etude in G Major

7.17

Fingerstyle Etude in a Flat Key

Below is a fingerstyle piece in the key of F Major. It is essentially in 5th position, however, at times, it moves briefly into 6th position. This piece includes many chord forms already covered in this book. Practice "Etude in F Major" slowly and accurately, being careful to connect the notes smoothly and allow them to ring out clearly; in other words, play the piece *legato*. Notice the curved lines above the notes—these are *phrase markings*, indicating the legato phrases.

Etude in F Major

7.18

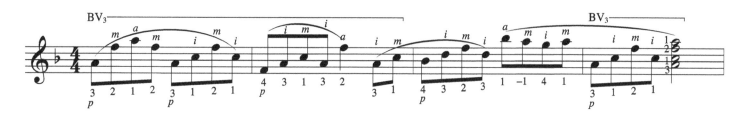

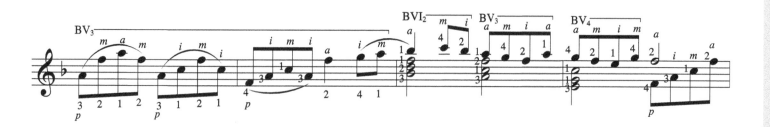

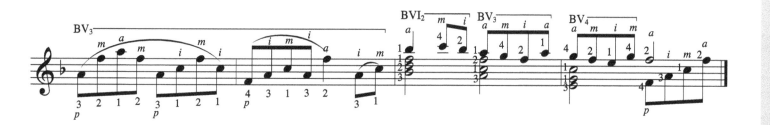

MAJOR TRIADS IN 5TH POSITION

As we continue moving up the neck of the guitar, it is important to become familiar with common major-triad fingerings in 5th position. When going through the voicings below, compare them to the voicings on page 22 to see how they have been transferred to this new position.

7.19

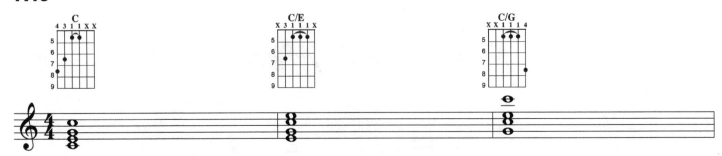

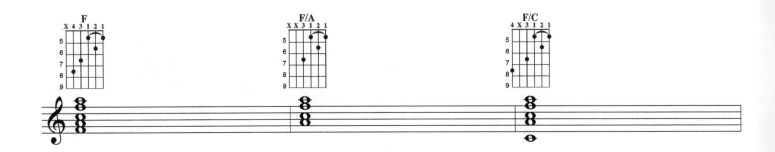

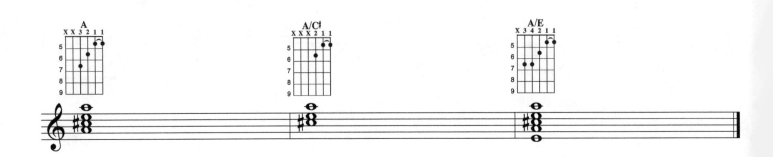

Minor Triads in 5th Position

Below are examples of minor-triad fingerings in 5th position. As you go through these shapes, compare them to the voicings on page 22 to see how they have been moved to this new position.

7.20

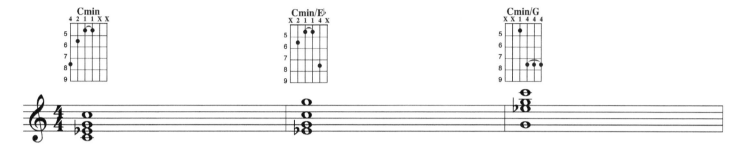

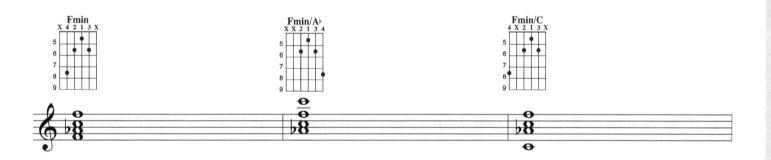

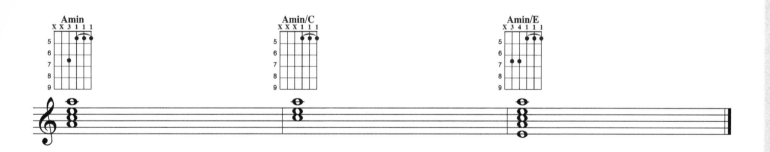

CHORD EXERCISE

Below is a sample piece featuring chord forms we learned on page 72, plus a few more. Practice strumming through these chords with the indicated rhythm.

Grooving in A

7.21

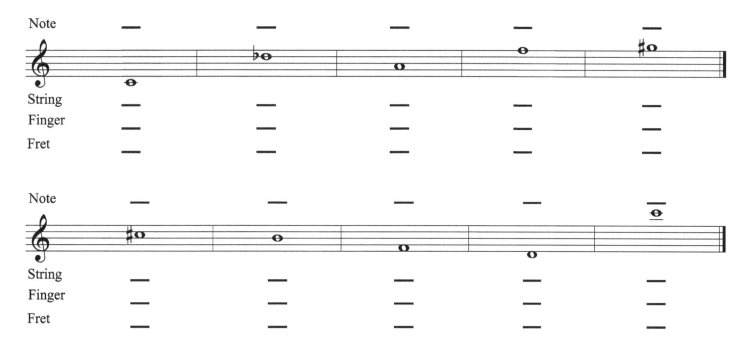

Guitar Legends: Jeff Beck

Profile
- Born in London, England on June 24, 1944
- Les Paul was the first electric guitar player who influenced him
- One of the most influential guitarists in rock
- Was introduced to Jimmy Page while both were teenagers
- Influenced by a wide variety of musicians, from Ravi Shankar to Django Reinhardt
- Ranked No. 5 in *Rolling Stone*'s list of the "100 Greatest Guitarists"

Style
- In his early years, Beck played with a pick, but beginning in the 1980s, he began to use his fingers exclusively
- Beck's guitar sound shaped many guitarists and styles that followed him, including heavy metal guitarists
- His guitar sound uses heavy distortion

Suggested Listening
- "Beck's Bolero"
- "Heart Full of Soul"
- "She's a Woman"
- "Going Down"

UNIT 8: 7TH CHORDS

Upon completion of this unit, the student will:

- Know the difference between minor triads and minor 7th chords
- Know the difference between major triads and dominant 7th chords
- Be able to play minor 7th chords as barre chords
- Be able to play dominant 7th chords as barre chords
- Be able to apply these chords to songs

So far, the chords we have looked at have been triads. As discussed earlier, triads are three-note chords. In this unit, we will expand our knowledge of chords by learning about *7th chords*. A 7th chord is a chord built off of a triad but contains one additional note, for a total of four notes.

The first type of 7th chord we'll look at is a *dominant 7th chord*. A dominant 7th chord consists of a major triad with a ♭7th. The chord symbol for a dominant 7th chord consists of the root name followed by "7."

8.1

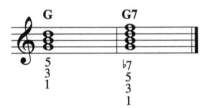

The next type of chord we'll learn is the *minor 7th chord*, which consists of a minor triad with a ♭7th. The chord symbol for this chord consists of the root name followed by "min7," as seen below.

8.2

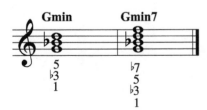

76 7th Chords ■ Unit 8

7TH CHORDS AS BARRE CHORDS

Now, let's look at barre-chord voicings for dominant and minor 7th chords.

Below are dominant 7th chords voiced as 6th-string and 5th-string barre chords. For comparison, we have also included the corresponding major-triad barre chords. This will help you better understand the difference between these two chords.

8.3

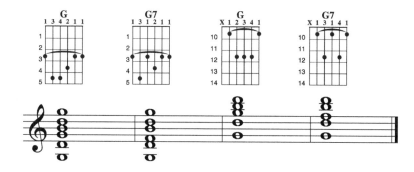

Next is a comparison between minor triads and minor 7th barre chords. Notice that by just changing one note in both of these examples, the chords take on a new character.

8.4

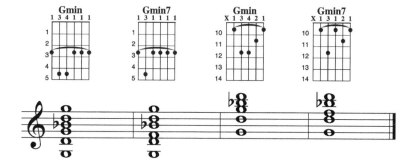

Below are practice tunes using various dominant 7th barre-chord forms. The first piece will help you change between barre chords more comfortably. Practice at a slow tempo and then speed it up as you become more accustomed to the chords.

Creek Fishin' Blues

8.5

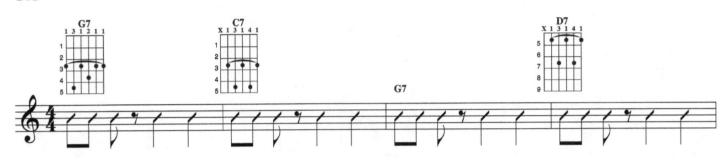

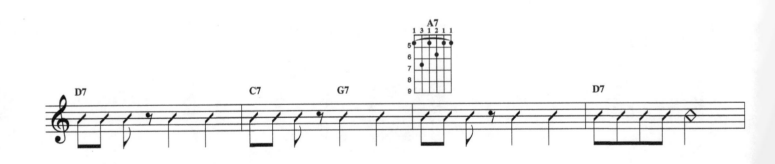

Half-Note Blues

8.6

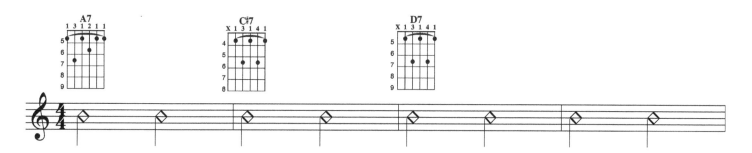
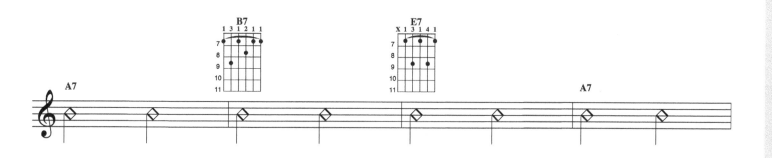
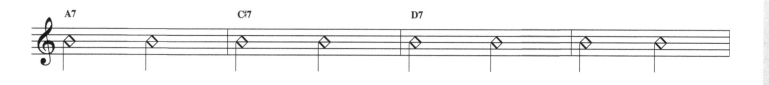

Unit 8   7th Chords

This next example uses various minor 7th barre-chord forms. It will get you changing between these voicings more comfortably. Having a good command of these voicings is essential to your playing. As with the previous example, practice this piece at a slow tempo, and then speed it up as you become more comfortable.

Doobie Do

8.7

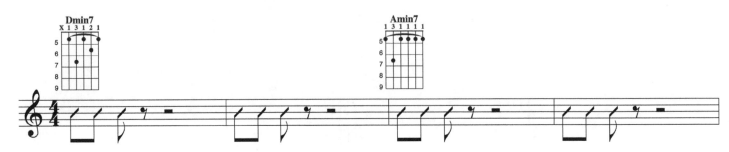

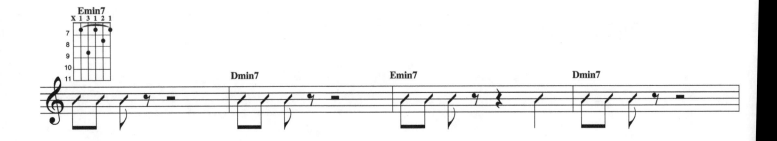

Below is another example featuring minor 7th barre chords, this time in a steady funk groove.

Minor Funk

8.8

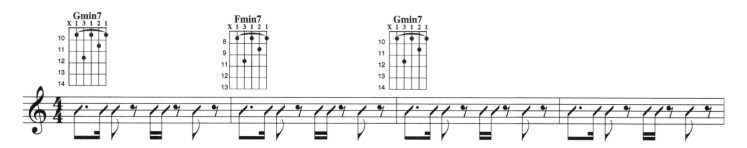

Now that we have learned barre-chord voicings for triads, minor 7ths, and dominant 7ths, we'll combine them in the piece below.

Minor Strut

8.9

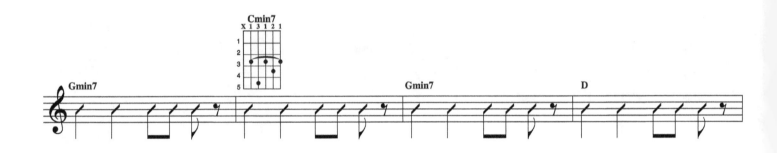

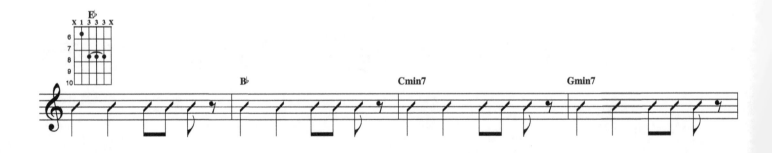

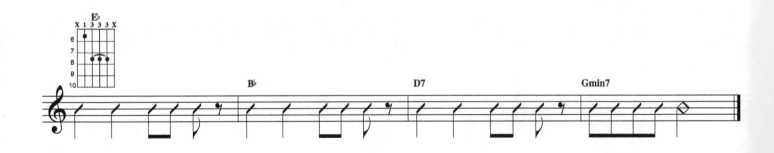

This next example also explores how we move between different types of barre chords. Be aware that many of these chords anticipate the beginning of the next measure by coming in an eighth note ahead.

Rockin' the Barre

8.10

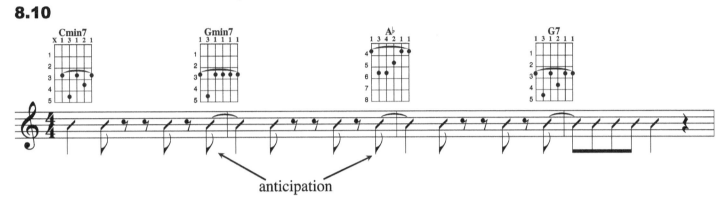

anticipation

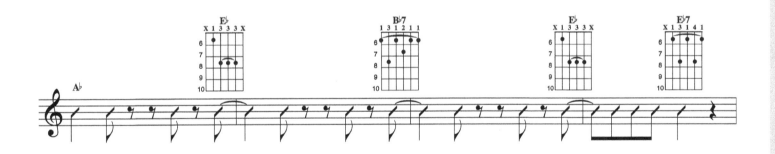

Unit 8 7th Chords 83

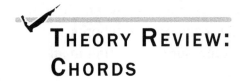
Theory Review: Chords

At this point, you have learned about major triads, minor triads, dominant 7th chords, and minor 7th chords. Below is a comparison of the contents of major and minor triads and 7th chords with a C root. Notice that the difference between the major and minor triad is the interval between the root and the third of the chord. When a minor 7th is added to these triads (in this case B♭), the result is a dominant 7th chord and a minor 7th chord, respectively.

8.11

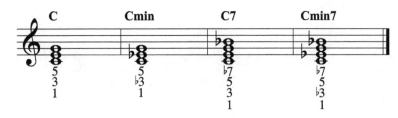

It is important to memorize the intervals above so you can start to identify chords more easily.

Time Test 8

In the examples below, identify each of the chords presented.

84   7th Chords   ■   Unit 8

Guitar Legends: John McLaughlin

Profile
- Born in Yorkshire, England
- Pioneering figure in the development of fusion music
- Performed with The Tony Williams Lifetime and Miles Davis
- Recorded on the Miles Davis albums *In a Silent Way*, *Bitches Brew*, *A Tribute to Jack Johnson*, and *On the Corner*
- Formed a pioneering fusion group called Mahavishnu Orchestra

Style
- Virtuoso guitarist
- Used rich harmonies and exotic scales in his compositions and improvisations
- Known for playing in complex time signatures
- Incorporated many different instruments in his playing, including the double-neck guitar and guitar synthesizer

Suggested Listening
- "Vital Transformation"
- "Meeting of the Spirits"
- "One Word"
- "Lotus Feet"

UNIT 9: MORE BLUES

OBJECTIVES

Upon completion of this unit, the student will:

- Know how to play different rhythm guitar patterns for the blues
- Know how to play the minor blues
- Be able to apply minor pentatonic and blues scale ideas in 5th position

BLUES PATTERNS UP THE NECK

In Unit 3, we played blues progressions using open strings. Now that we are becoming more familiar with the notes in 5th position (and higher), we are going to take those same progressions and apply them to this area of the guitar. Playing these progressions will require some stretches with the pinky.

In this first progression, the 1st finger stays down while the 3rd finger alternates with the 4th finger a whole step higher. TAB is included in the following examples to help you learn this approach quicker.

9.1

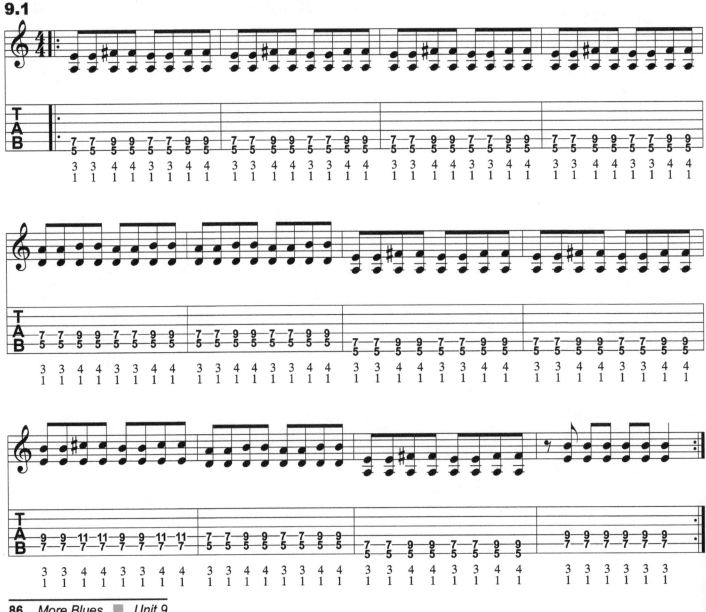

This next example is similar to the previous one, but it requires a stretch with the pinky so you can reach the ♭7th of each chord.

9.2

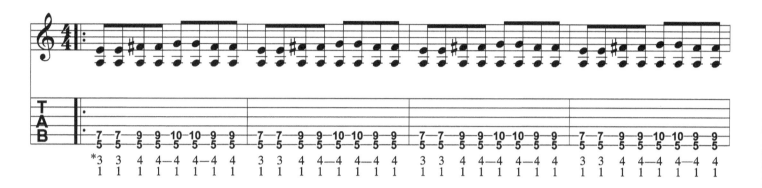

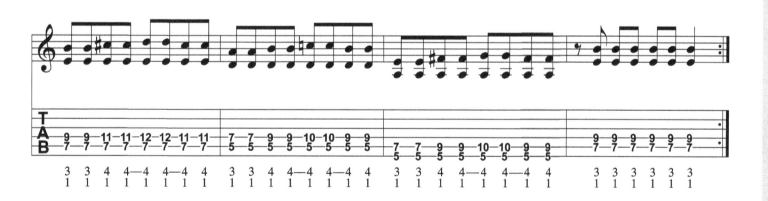

* You may find it more comfortable to use your 2nd finger instead of the 3rd finger in this example.

In the example below, we are combining dominant 7th barre chords and a moving single-note line. This is a classic blues rhythm-guitar pattern and is to be played with a swing, or shuffle, feel.

9.3

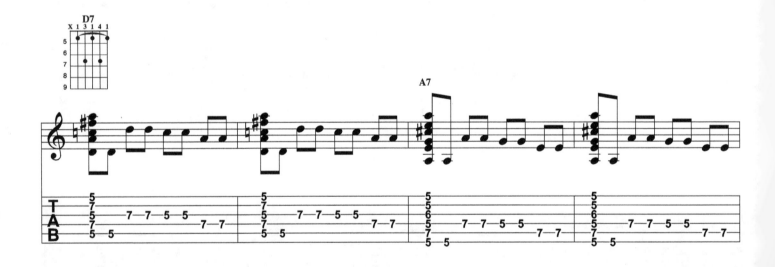

The following example uses barre chords and elements of Example 9.1 to create an interesting blues rhythm-guitar part.

9.4

Minor Blues

The blues progressions we have learned so far have included major triads, power chords, and dominant 7th chords. In all of these cases, the I–IV–V progression remained consistent. The next type of blues we will look at is the *minor blues*, which is a blues progression made up entirely (or almost entirely) of minor chords. In our first example, our chords still follow a I–IV–V pattern, but instead of major or dominant 7th chords, we are playing minor chords built on the 1st, 4th, and 5th degrees of the minor scale. Note that lowercase Roman numerals are used for minor chords: i–iv–v.

9.5

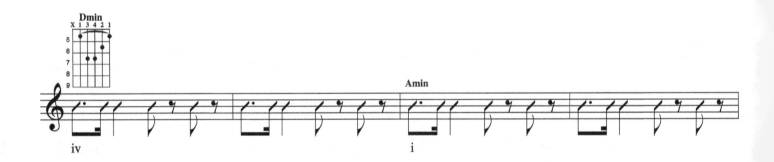

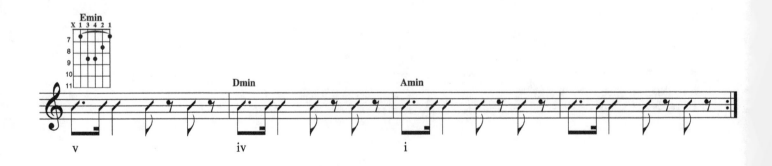

This next example uses minor 7th chords in the same way we used minor triads in the previous example. Let's look at some ways that this example differs from the previous one. In measure 9, instead of the expected V chord, Emin7, we see an F triad. This commonly happens in a minor blues because the F triad is *diatonic* in this key. This means that all of the notes of the chord come from the key the piece is in. On page 87 of *Guitar 101*, Book 1, we learned the notes that are in a natural minor scale. If you were to build triads on each of those notes in A Minor, you would get the following:

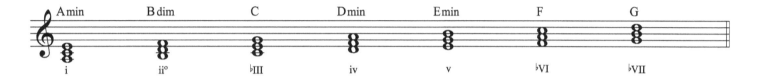

In terms of Roman numerals, the F major is the ♭VI chord, as it is built off of the 6th degree of the A Natural Minor scale.

Another difference in this next example is in measure 10. Here, instead of the IV chord, Dmin, we have an E7 chord. This is the V7 chord in this key. We borrow this chord from the A *Harmonic Minor scale*. A harmonic minor scale is a natural minor scale with the 7th degree raised a half step. In this case, the G is raised to a G♯. E7 appears in the final measure as well.

9.6

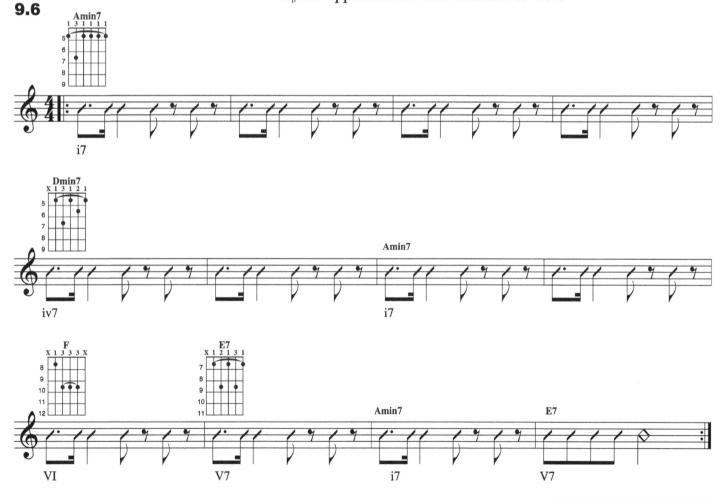

Unit 9 ■ More Blues 91

Improvising in 5th Position

The two scales we have been learning to improvise with have been the A Minor Pentatonic scale and the A Blues scale. Let's look at the fingerings for these scales in 5th position.

9.7—A Minor Pentatonic Scale

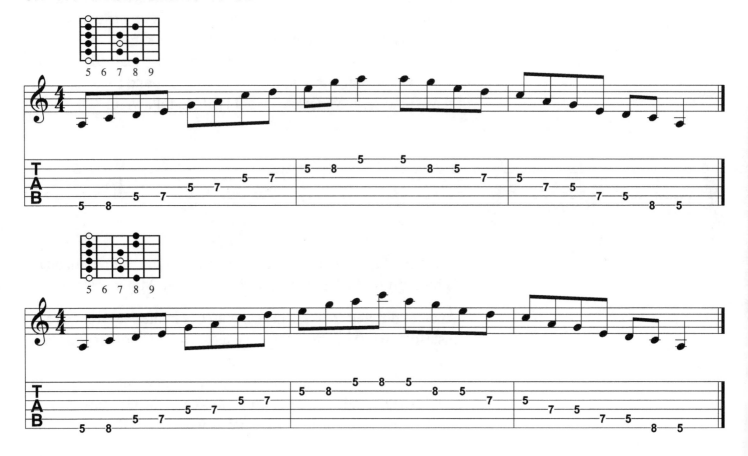

9.8—A Blues Scale

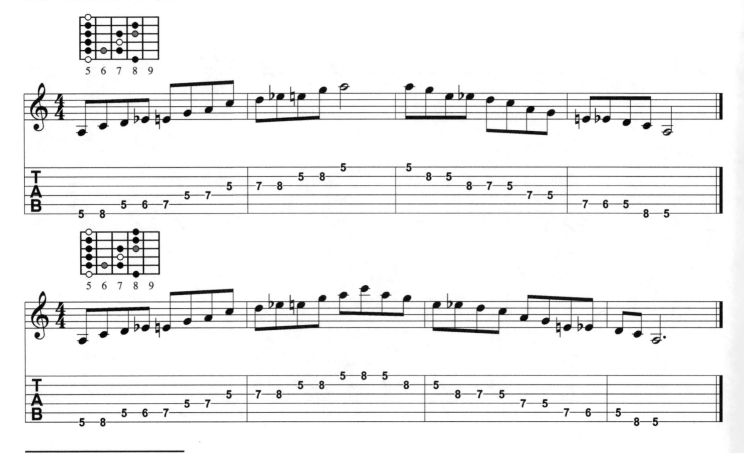

A Minor Pentatonic Ideas

Following are ideas derived from the A Minor Pentatonic scale. These ideas can be used to improvise over all of the blues examples in this chapter. Here is the pattern from which these licks are derived:

9.9

9.10

9.11

Below are some ideas derived from the A Blues scale. These can be used to improvise over all of the blues examples in this chapter. To the right is the pattern from which these licks are derived.

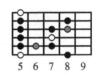

9.12

9.13

9.14

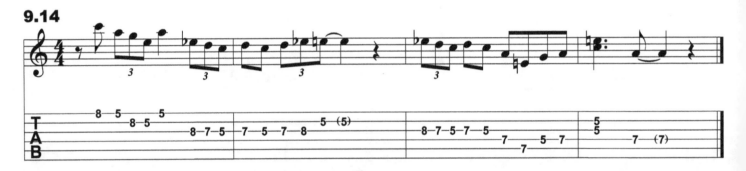

Learn the examples above and practice playing them over the various blues examples found in this chapter.

Identify the following chords.

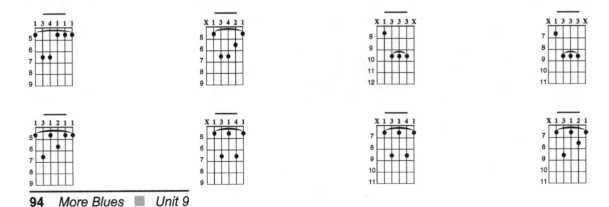

Guitar Legends: Buddy Guy

Profile
- Born in Lettsworth, Louisiana
- Moved to Chicago in the early 1950s
- Once in Chicago, Guy became influenced by the music of Muddy Waters
- Helped define the sound of Chicago blues
- Member of Rock and Roll Hall of Fame

Style
- Used distortion and feedback in his sound
- Began playing longer solos that had greater dynamic shifts
- Loud and aggressive style of playing
- Incorporated lessons learned from other guitarists, including Muddy Waters, Howlin' Wolf, and Guitar Slim

Suggested Listening
- "Messin' with the Kid"
- "Hoodoo Man Blues"
- "I Got My Eyes on You"
- "Can't Quit the Blues"

UNIT 10: INTRODUCTION TO 7TH POSITION

OBJECTIVES

Upon completion of this unit, the student will:

- Be able to perform single-note melodies in 7th position in multiple keys
- Know major scales in 7th position
- Know major and minor triads in 7th position
- Be able to read monophonic music in 7th position in multiple keys
- Be able to read polyphonic music in 7th position in multiple keys

SCALES IN 7TH POSITION

Let's begin our study of 7th position by looking at the natural notes found in this location. As we did in units 2 and 7, we will begin our introduction of 7th position with the C Major scale. TAB is included in these examples to get you accustomed to playing in this position.

10.1

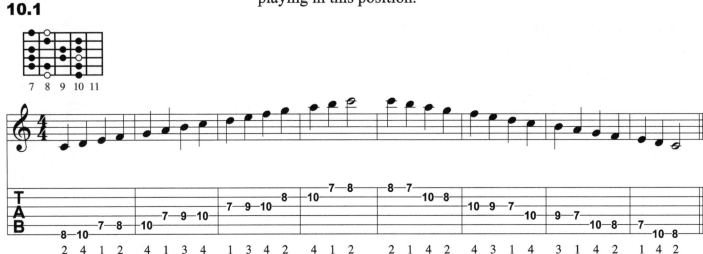

If we look at all the natural notes found in 7th position, we actually get the exact same notes as above, but we add one note above (D) and one note below (B).

10.2

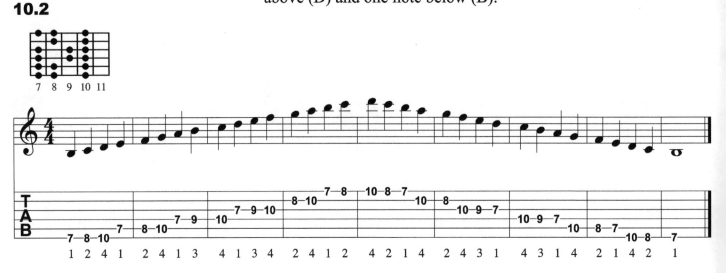

10.3

Below is an example with all the chromatic notes in 7th position. When ascending, the non-natural notes are represented with sharps, and when descending, they are represented as flats.

Major Scales in 7th Position

Below are fingerings for major scales in 7th position. Learning these major scales will help you gain a better understanding of the notes in this position. Practice these scales below and make sure you are reading the notes. This will reinforce your fretboard knowledge and help you become a better sight-reader.

10.4—C Major Scale in 7th Position

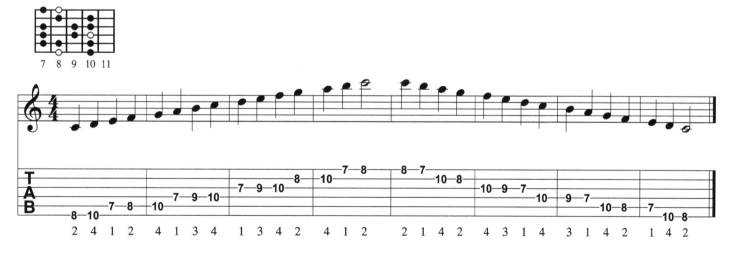

10.5—F Major Scale in 7th Position

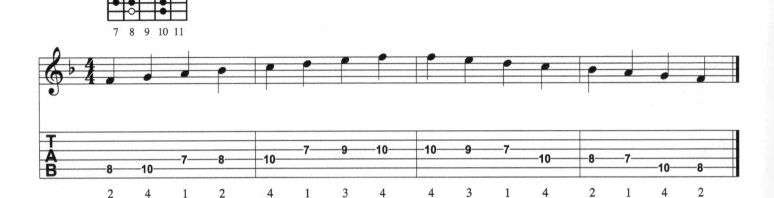

10.6—G Major Scale in 7th Position

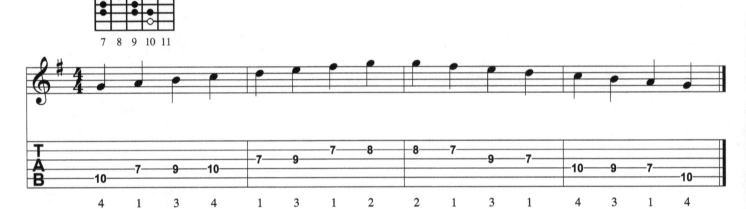

10.7—A Major Scale in 7th Position

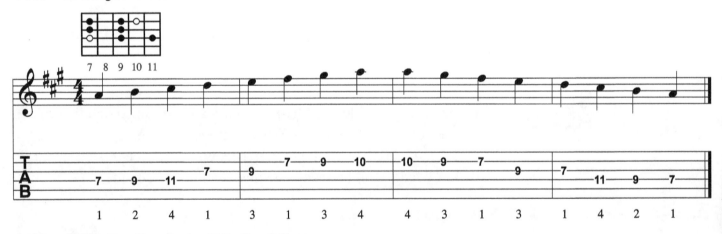

10.8—D Major Scale in 7th Position

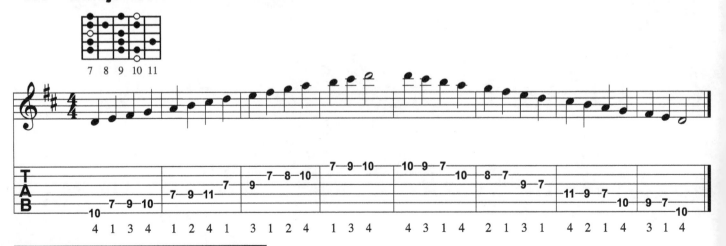

Melodic Etudes

Below are brief etudes in the keys of the major scales covered on the previous pages. Practice sight-reading these etudes either pickstyle or fingerstyle. To reinforce your reading skills, no TAB is included for these etudes. Use the fingerings of the corresponding major scales to play these etudes.

10.9—Etude in F Major

10.10—Etude in D Major

10.11—Etude in A Major

10.12—Etude in G Major

Below is an etude that can be played fingerstyle or pickstyle. This piece utilizes chords in 7th position. Paying close attention to the indicated fingerings will help you remain in position.

Harmonic Etude I

10.13

Here is another etude that can be played fingerstyle or pickstyle. This piece is entirely in 7th position. Be mindful of the indicated fingerings to help you stay in position.

Harmonic Etude 2

10.14

* This indicates that you should hold this note to allow it ring as long as possible.

Major Triads in 7th and 8th Position

Following are major triad voicings in 7th and 8th position. Compare them to the voicings on pages 22 and 73 to see how they have been moved to this new position.

10.15

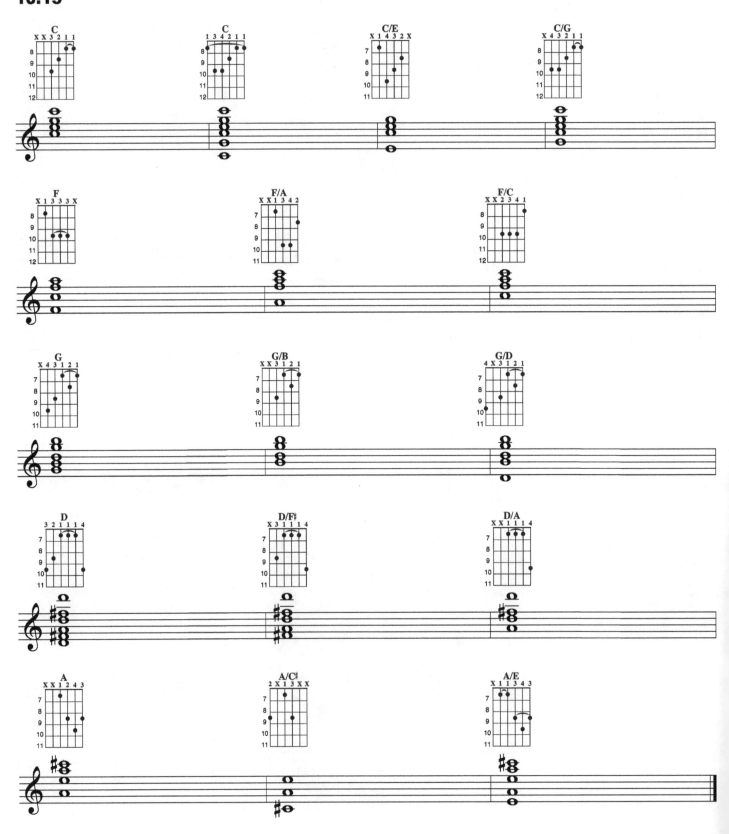

Minor Triads in 7th and 8th Position

Below are minor triad voicings in 7th and 8th position. Notice the relationship between these chords and the ones on page 102. This will help you see the differences between major and minor triads in a single position.

10.16

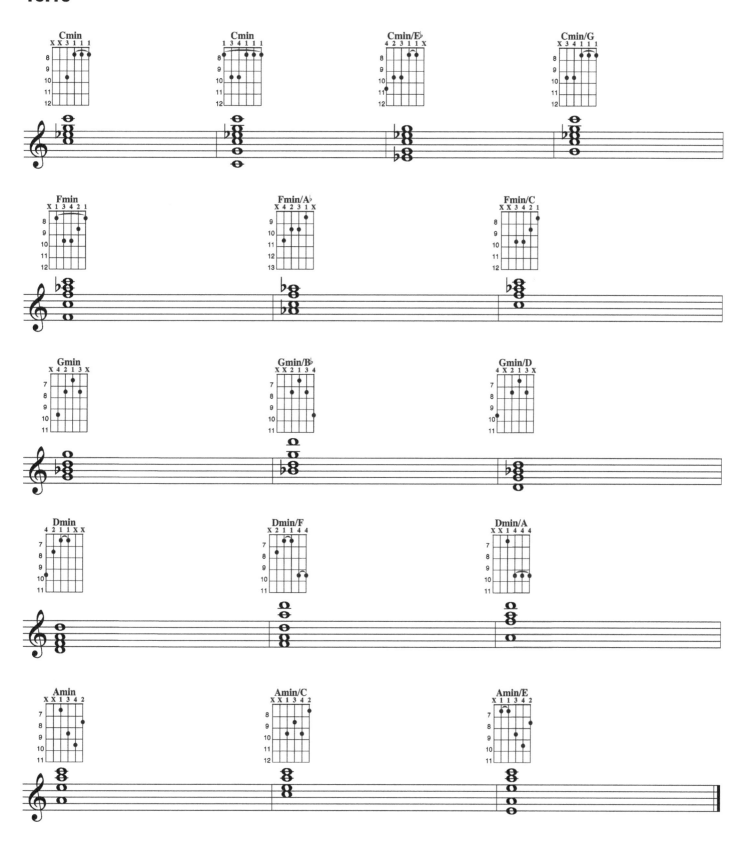

Unit 10 — Introduction to 7th Position

STRUMMING ETUDES

The following examples will help you practice strumming chords in the 7th and 8th positions. The rhythms are somewhat repetitive to allow you to focus on making the chord changes smoothly and accurately.

10.17

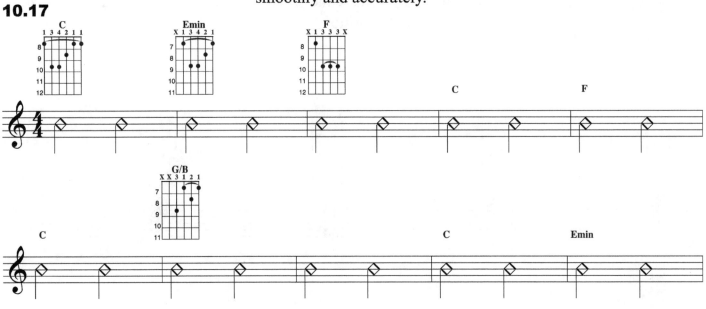

This next example has a reggae feel.

10.18

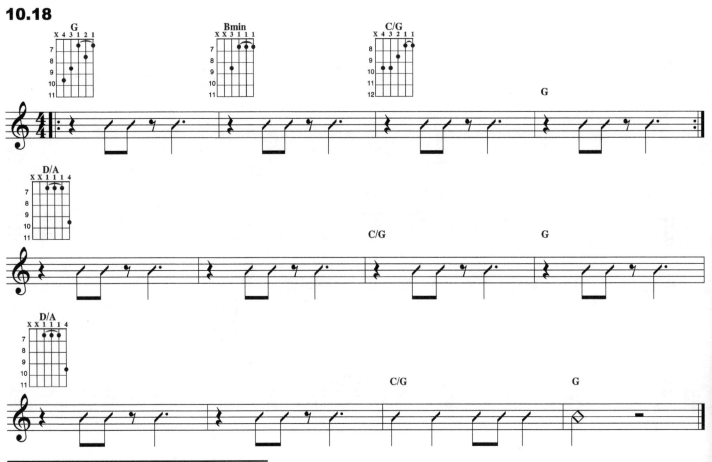

Time Test 10

Identify the following notes in 7th position.

Note	—	—	—	—	—
String	—	—	—	—	—
Finger	—	—	—	—	—
Fret	—	—	—	—	—

Note	—	—	—	—	—
String	—	—	—	—	—
Finger	—	—	—	—	—
Fret	—	—	—	—	—

Guitar Legends: Ernest Ranglin

Profile
- Born in 1932 in Manchester, Jamaica
- Learned to play from guitar books, by imitating his uncles, and attending late-night jam sessions in Jamaica
- Influenced by traditional music from Jamaica and big band artists like Duke Ellington, Stan Kenton, and Benny Goodman
- Session guitarist for Studio One Records and Island Records
- Worked with many important reggae artists, including Bob Marley, Jimmy Cliff, and Prince Buster

Style
- One of the founding fathers of the ska rhythm-guitar style
- Blends together jazz, calypso, mento, reggae, and rhythm & blues influences into his sound
- Rhythmic style of playing, with jazz and blues nuances
- First rhythm guitarist to use more complex chords in reggae and ska

Suggested Listening
- "Easy Snapping"
- "My Boy Lollipop"
- "Up on the Downstroke"
- "Surfin'"

UNIT 11: MINOR PENTATONIC AND BLUES SCALES— 7TH POSITION AND MULTIPLE-POSITION FINGERINGS

OBJECTIVES

Upon completion of this unit, the student will:

- Know how to play the A Minor Pentatonic and A Blues scale in 7th position
- Know how to play A Minor Pentatonic and A Blues scale licks in 7th position
- Be able to play multiple-position fingerings for the A Minor Pentatonic and A Blues scales
- Be able to play a blues melody in multiple positions

BASIC FINGERINGS IN 7TH POSITION

As we continue our study of the 7th position, let's check out the A Minor Pentatonic and A Blues scales. Below are two fingerings for each of these scales in 7th position. The first version is a one-octave fingering, and the second contains all of the scale's notes found in the 7th position. In these examples, the scale returns to the tonic, A, so that we hear the notes in relation to the tonic. Practice both versions of these scales. TAB is included so you can quickly become familiar with this new material.

11.1—A Minor Pentatonic Scale

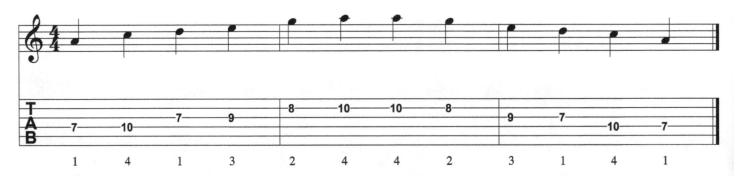

11.2

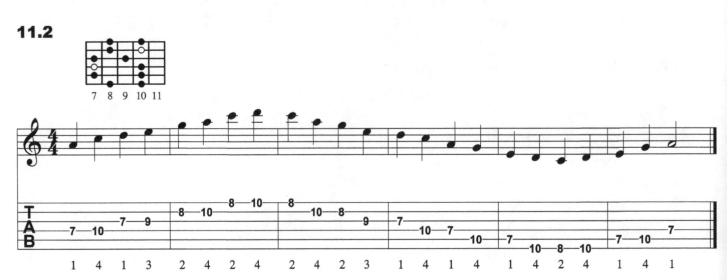

11.3—A Blues Scale

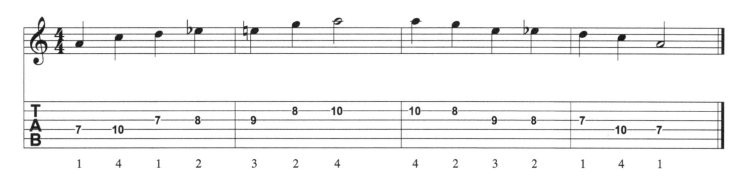

11.4

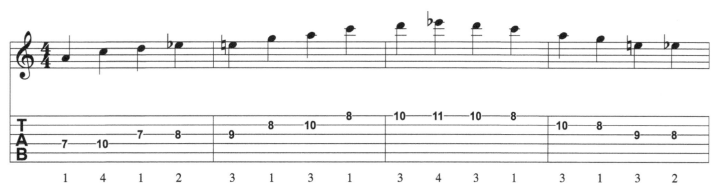
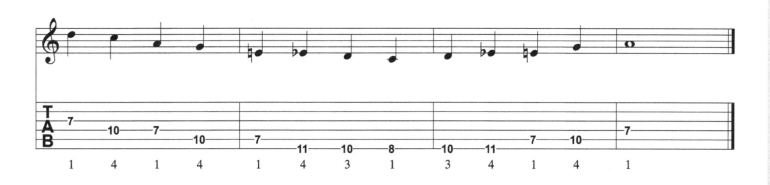

A Minor Pentatonic Ideas

The following four examples are A Minor Pentatonic ideas that can be used in improvisation. Learn these licks using the 7th position fingerings learned on page 106.

11.5
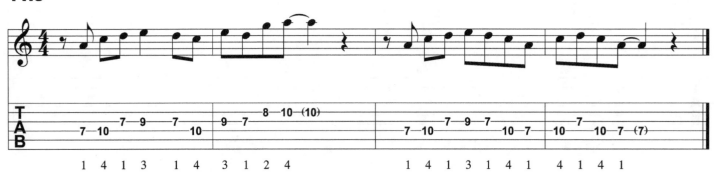

11.6
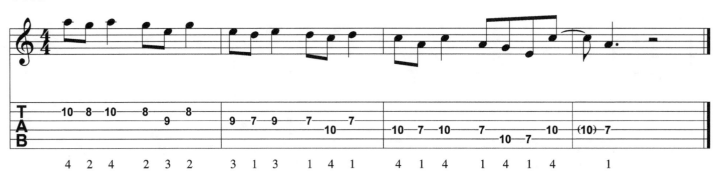

11.7

11.8
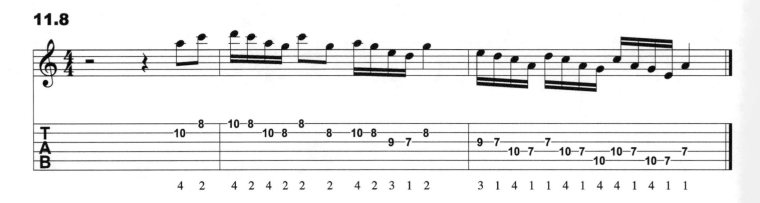

A Blues Scale Ideas

Below are four examples of A Blues scale ideas that can be used in improvisation. Learn these licks and connect them to the fingerings on page 107.

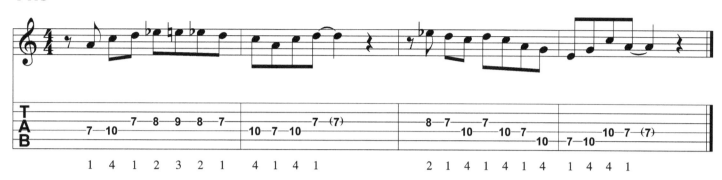

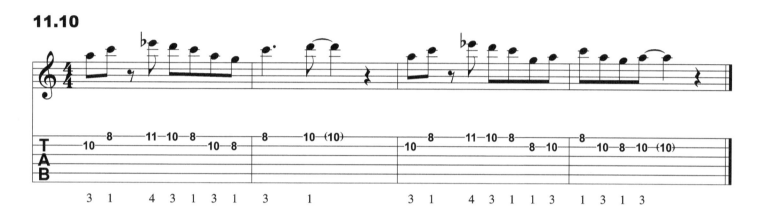

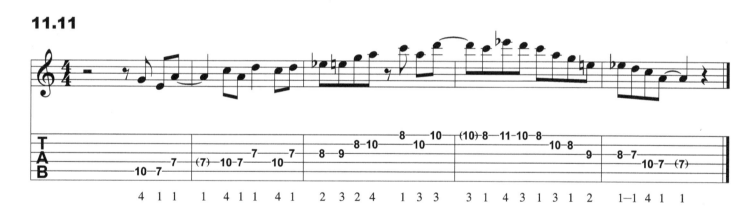

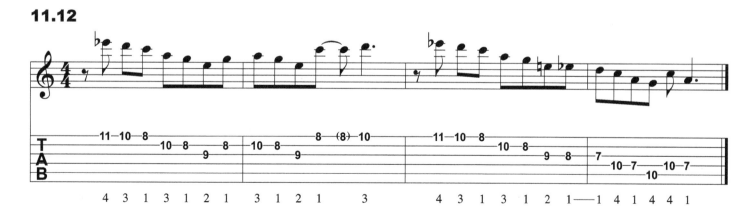

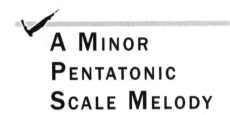

A Minor Pentatonic Scale Melody

Below is a melody composed of notes from the A Minor Pentatonic scale. Notice that the melody consists of three similar phrases, each of which is four measures long. Be aware of the differences between the three phrases. The rhythm for each four-bar phrase is the same, though the notes change. Throughout, we continue to use notes from the A Minor Pentatonic scale, but the note choices change ever so slightly. The consistency of the four-measure rhythm is known as a *motif*—a short melodic, harmonic, or rhythmic phrase that repeats. It is a common practice to build a melody using motifs, which is what we are doing in Example 11.13.

11.13

Exercises

1. Divide the class into two groups. Have one group play the melody above while the other group plays a rhythm-guitar part from Unit 6.
2. While the class is playing the chords, have each student improvise using motifs and the melody above as a starting point.

A Blues Scale Melody

Next is a melody composed of notes from the A Blues Scale. Like the previous example, this melody is made up of three similar phrases, each of which is four measures long. Be aware of the differences between the three phrases. Playing a melody in this fashion is known as *call and response*. The first two measures of each four-bar phrase are the same, but the last two bars are different. The first two represent the "call," and the last two represent the "response." This technique is common in blues music and is something you should become familiar with as you begin to understand how the blues is constructed.

11.14

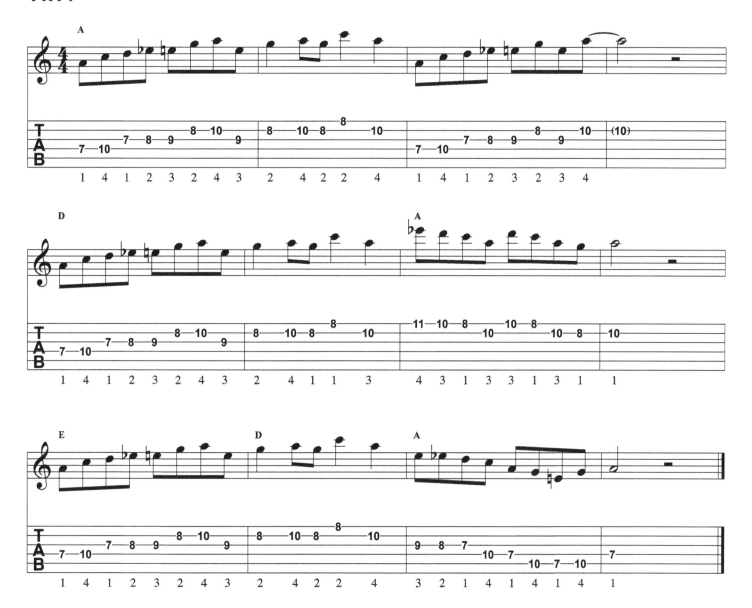

Exercise

1. Divide the class into two groups. Have one group play the melody above while the other group plays a rhythm-guitar part from Unit 6.
2. While the class is playing the chords, have each student improvise using call and response and the melody above as a starting point.

Multiple-Position A Minor Pentatonic Scale

In this section, we are going to combine the fingering for the A Minor Pentatonic scale in 5th position with the one in 7th position. To do this, we have to make a calculated *shift* (the movement from one position to another) to avoid a break in the sound as our hand moves up the fretboard. Notice in the example below that the shift occurs when we move our 1st finger from the G on the 4th string in 5th position to the A on the 4th string in 7th position. Practice this the two ways presented: first as a two-octave fingering (11.15), then ascending to the highest note from that scale in 7th position, D, and returning back to the tonic, A (11.16).

11.15

11.16

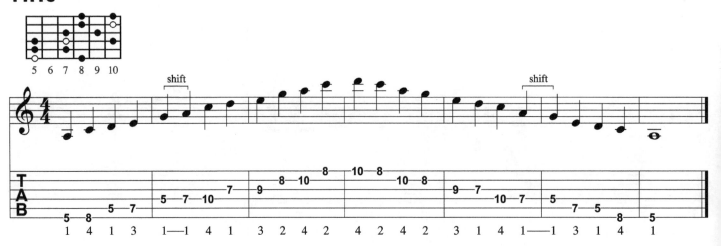

Multiple-Position A Blues Scale

Next, we will combine the fingering for the A Blues Scale in 5th position with the one in 7th position. The fingering here corresponds to the fingering used for the A Minor Pentatonic scale on the previous page. As you practice these fingerings, notice the similarities and differences between the pentatonic and the blues-scale fingerings. Practice these scales in the two ways presented: first as a two-octave fingering, then ascending to a high E♭ at the 11th fret.

Multi-Position Blues Melody

Following is a blues melody written using a combination of the multi-position A Minor Pentatonic and A Blues scales introduced on the previous two pages. Practice this with accompaniment and use elements of this melody to construct your own blues improvisations.

11.19

Time Test 11

Write out the fingering in the TAB for the following line in 7th position.

Guitar Legends: Kenny Burrell

Profile
- Born in 1931 in Detroit, Michigan
- Influenced by Charlie Christian, Django Reinhardt, and Wes Montgomery
- Began his performing career as a member of The Dizzy Gillespie Sextet while still a student at Wayne State University
- Performed as a sideman for many established artists, including Jimmy Smith, Stanley Turrentine, Shirley Scott, and John Coltrane
- Faculty member at UCLA teaching "Ellingtonia"—a retrospective of the life and music of Duke Ellington

Style
- Grounded in the blues
- Known for tasteful, melodic, and elegant soloing style
- Associated with both hard bop and soul jazz genres
- Well-respected solo guitarist

Suggested Listening
- "Chitlins Con Carne"
- "Freight Trane"
- "Back at the Chicken Shack"
- "Midnight Blue"

UNIT 12: INTRODUCTION TO 9TH AND 10TH POSITION

OBJECTIVES

Upon completion of this unit, the student will:

- Perform single-note melodies in 9th and 10th position in multiple keys
- Be able to play major scales in 9th and 10th position
- Be able to play major and minor triads in 9th and 10th position
- Be able to read monophonic music in 9th and 10th position in multiple keys
- Be able to read polyphonic music in 9th and 10th position in multiple keys

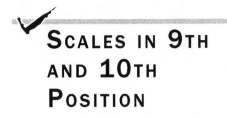

SCALES IN 9TH AND 10TH POSITION

In this unit, we will study the notes in the 9th and 10th positions. We refer to "9th and 10th position" because the natural notes in this location of the fretboard can be reached from either position. From 9th position, we will just need to shift when we cross between the 3rd and 2nd strings. From 10th position, we will need to stretch the 4th finger to the note E on the 4th string at the 14th fret. Both of these fingerings are represented below.

12.1

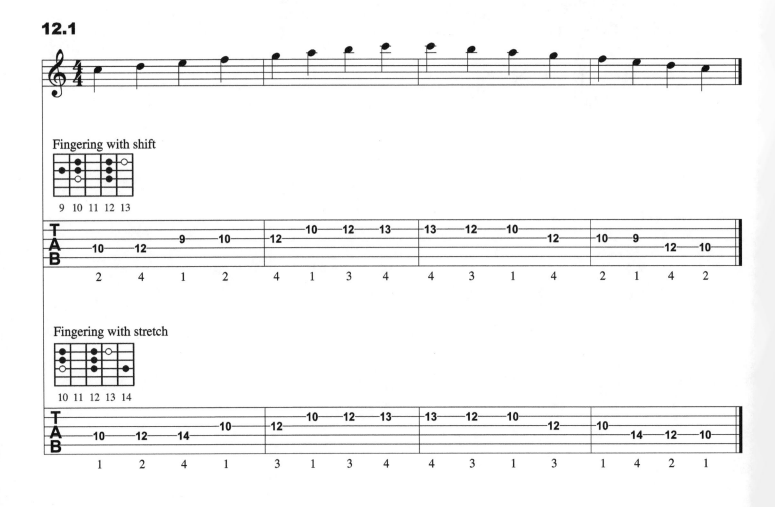

Below are all the natural notes found in 9th and 10th position. Regardless of where we start, we get the same notes. Both fingerings are represented here in standard notation, fretboard diagrams, and TAB.

12.2

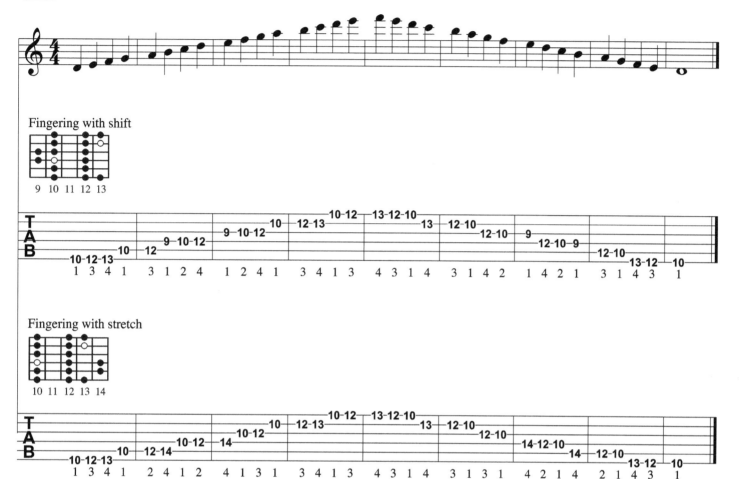

Below is an example that includes all of the natural and non-natural notes in 9th and 10th position. Remember, the ascending non-natural notes are represented with sharps, while the descending non-natural notes are represented with flats. Two fingerings are included, one in 9th position and one in 10th. Note that the fingering in 10th position, technically, begins and ends in 9th position. Try saying the note names aloud as you practice these fingerings.

12.3

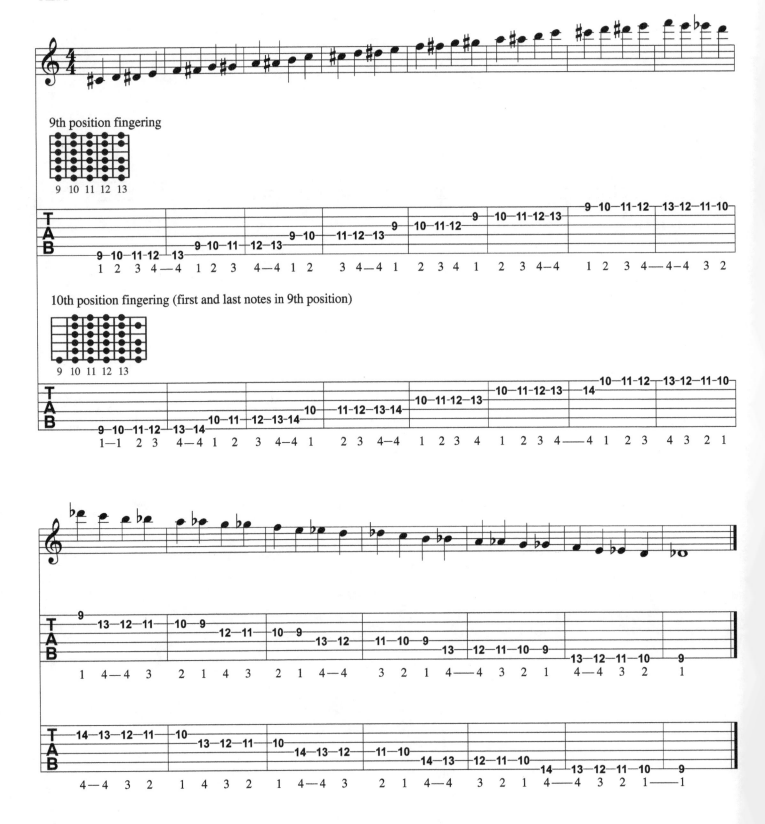

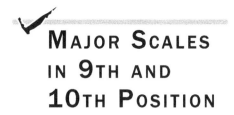

Major Scales in 9th and 10th Position

Following are fingerings for major scales in 9th and 10th position. With the inclusion of the fingering learned for the C Major scale found on page 116, you have now learned the five single-position fingerings for major scales (shown in Example 12.4)

12.4—The Five Single-Position Major-Scale Fingerings

See if you can identify these scale patterns as you play through the scales below.

12.5—F Major Scale

(Note: If you move this scale down a half step, you get a 9th-position E Major scale.)

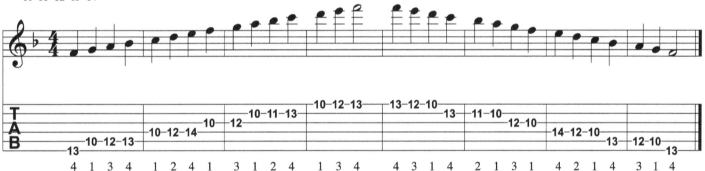

12.6—D Major Scale

12.7—G Major Scale

12.8—B♭ Major Scale

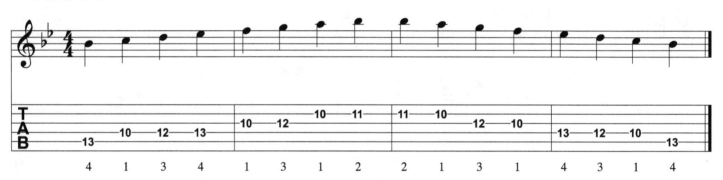

12.9—B Major Scale

As we have moved up the neck and studied all the major and chromatic scales:

1. We have learned all the notes from the open strings to the 13th fret.
2. We have learned that the major scale has five basic, single-position fingerings.

See if you can identify these shapes in the scales on pages 119 and 120. In doing so, you will gain an even greater understanding of the fretboard.

MELODIC ETUDES

Below are etudes in keys of selected major scales from the previous pages. You can play these etudes with a pick or fingerstyle. Try these without TAB to make sure you are learning the locations of the notes.

12.10—Etude in F Major

12.11—Etude in D Major

12.12—Etude in G Major

12.13—Etude in E Major

Below is a fingerstyle etude played in a combination of 9th and 10th positions. Pay close attention to the indicated fingerings, as this will lead you to common chord voicings found in previous chapters.

Fingerstyle Etude in 9th and 10th

12.14

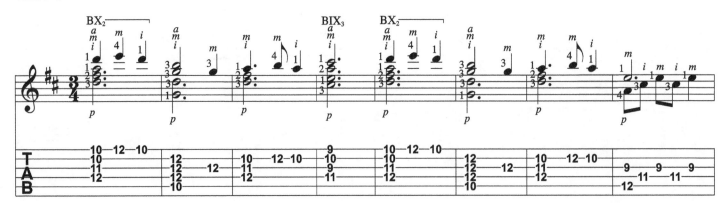

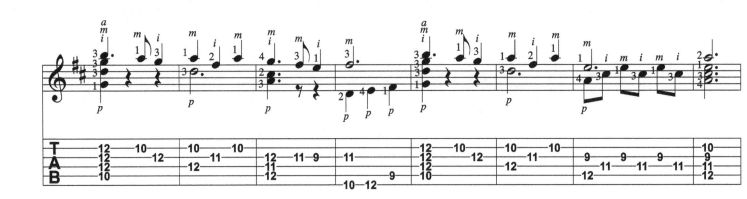

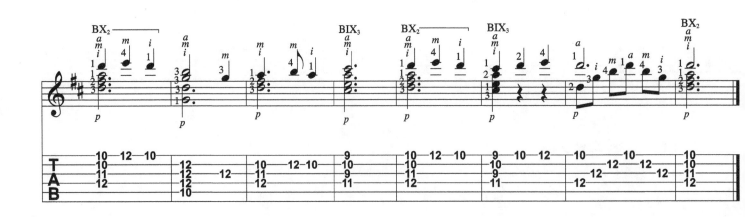

Major and Minor Triads in 9th and 10th Position

Below are major and minor triad voicings in 9th and 10th position. Practice these slowly, noting the similarities to other voicings presented throughout this book. (In other words, notice that they are the same voicings but moved to this new location.)

12.15

Below are a couple of etudes to practice strumming chords in 9th and 10th position. The rhythms change subtly, so make sure you pay close attention to the notation.

12.16

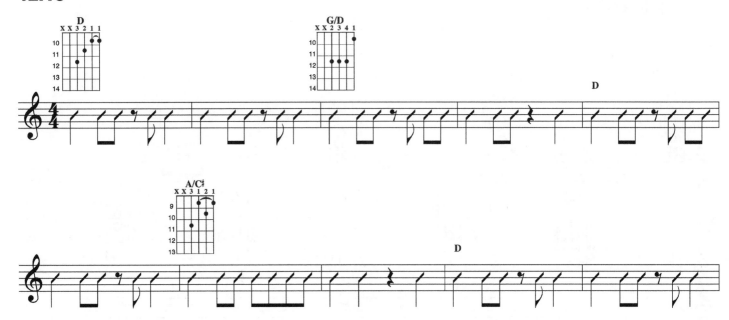

12.17

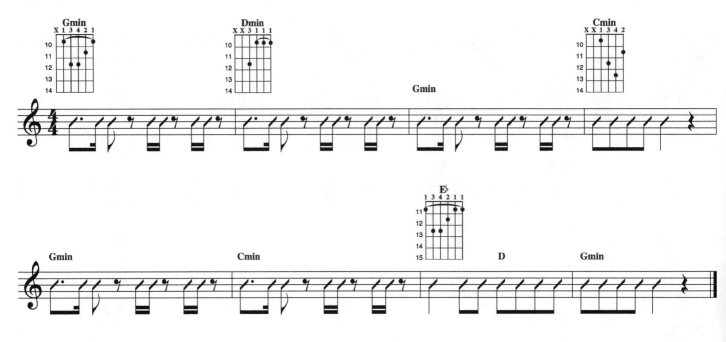

Time Test 12

Identify the following notes in 9th position.

[Musical staff with notes to identify, with blank lines for Note, String, Finger, and Fret for each of 5 notes in two rows]

Guitar Legends: Eddie Van Halen

Profile
- Born on January 26, 1955 in Nijmegen, Holland
- Began his musical pursuits as an accomplished pianist, winning awards as a child
- Switched to guitar after hearing "Wipe Out" by The Surfaris, and because he was bored with piano
- Influenced by Eric Clapton and Jimmy Page
- Co-founder of the famous hard rock band Van Halen
- Listed as one of the "100 Greatest Guitarists" in both *Rolling Stone* (#8) and *Guitar World* (#1) magazines

Style
- Virtuosic guitar technique
- Master of two-handed tapping, harmonics, vibrato, and tremolo-picking styles
- Solos are considered masterpieces of rock guitar
- Played a "Frankenstrat" guitar, which he assembled from parts of multiple guitars

Suggested Listening
- "Eruption"
- "Panama"
- "Hot for Teacher"
- "Everybody Wants Some"

UNIT 13: MINOR PENTATONIC AND BLUES SCALES—9TH/10TH POSITION AND MULTIPLE-POSITION FINGERINGS

OBJECTIVES

Upon completion of this unit, the student will:

- Be able to play A Minor Pentatonic and A Blues scales in 9th/10th position
- Be able to play A Minor Pentatonic and A Blues ideas in 9th/10th position
- Be able to play multiple-position fingerings for the A Minor Pentatonic and A Blues scales
- Be able to play a blues melody in multiple positions

SCALE FINGERINGS IN 9TH/10TH POSITION

In this unit, we will begin by looking at the A Minor Pentatonic and A Blues scales in 9th/10th position. We are referring to it as "9th/10th position" because part of each fingering is in 9th position and part of it is in 10th. Following are two fingerings for each scale. In order to play these fingerings, we need to incorporate a shift when moving from the 3rd string to the 2nd string. The first version of each scale is a one-octave fingering, and the second includes all the notes from that scale in 9th/10th position. Practice both versions of these scales, always returning to the tonic, A.

13.1—A Minor Pentatonic Scale

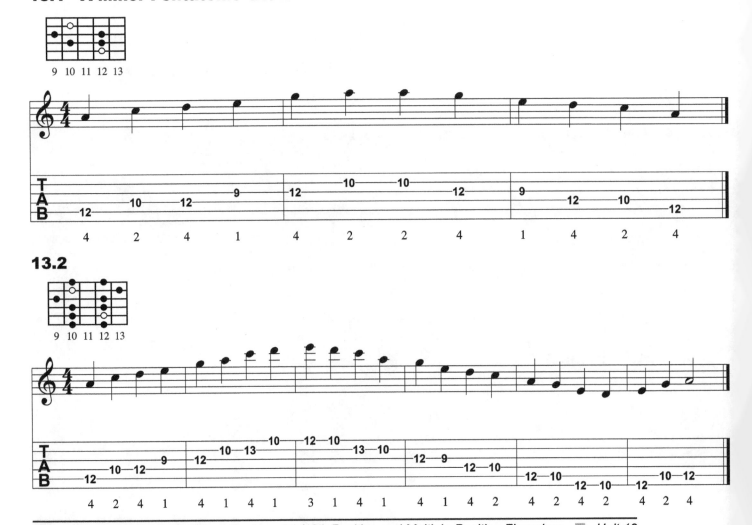

13.3—A Blues Scale

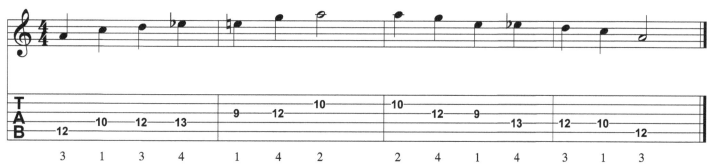

13.4

Unit 13 Minor Pentatonic and Blues Scales—9th/10th Position and Multiple-Position Fingerings

A Minor Pentatonic Scale Ideas in 9th/10th Position

Below are some ideas derived from the A Minor Pentatonic scale in 9th/10th position. Practice playing these licks over some of the blues accompaniments from earlier units in this book.

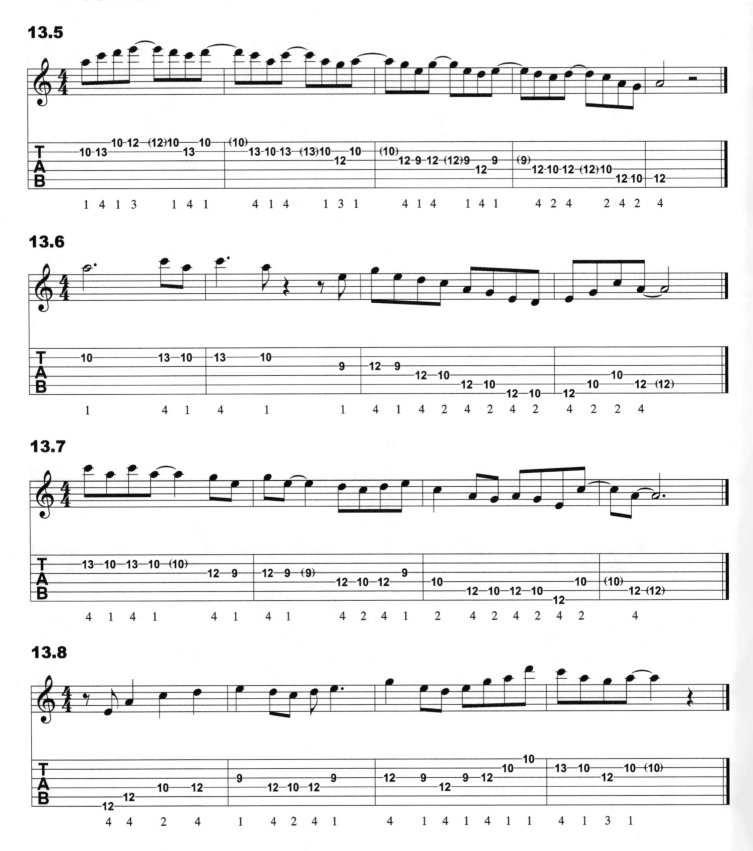

A Blues Scale Ideas in 9th/10th Position

Following are some licks and ideas that come from the A Blues scale in 9th/10th position. These will work great over a blues progression in A.

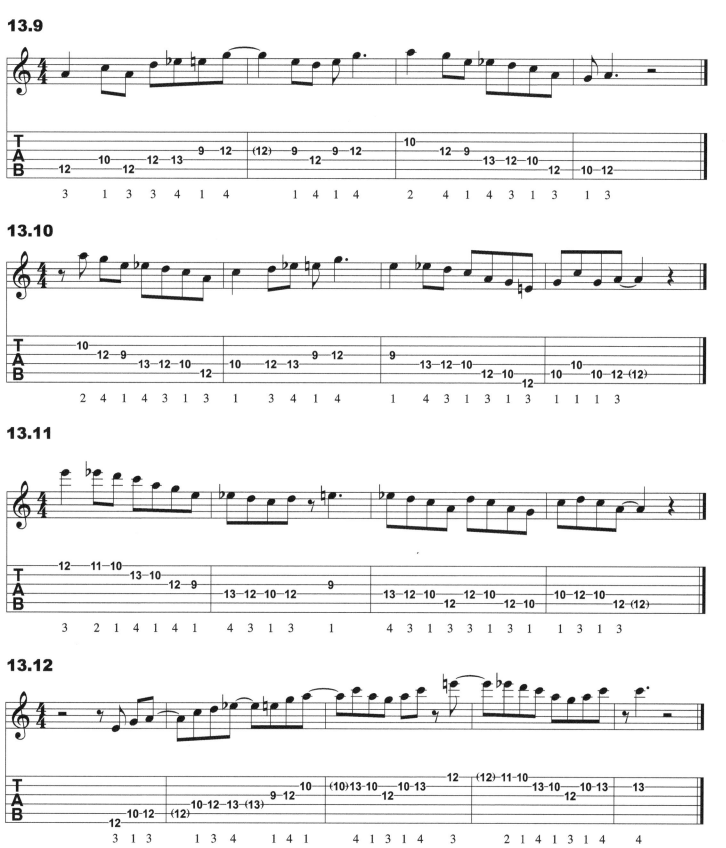

Blues Melody Using the A Minor Pentatonic Scale

Below is a melody written from the notes of the A Minor Pentatonic scale. This melody includes motifs and is played in the 9th/10th position. Additionally, it should be played with a swing feel.

13.13

Blues Melody Using the A Blues Scale

Below is a melody written from the notes of the A Blues scale. Pay attention to the different rhythmic motifs throughout the example. We begin with a four-bar phrase that features a repetitive rhythmic motif. The next four bars consist of two, two-bar phrases that have a similar rhythmic composition. The last four bars are the response and close out this piece. Seeing, hearing, and practicing phrase structure can help you understand songs and learn them more quickly. When approaching this piece, practice the phrases separately and then put them all together.

13.14

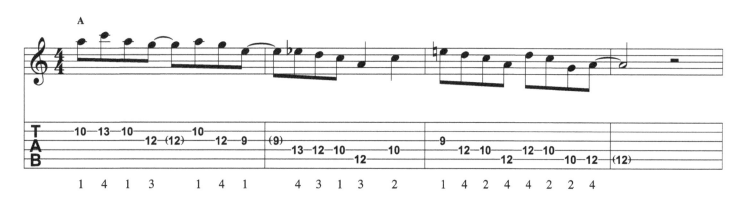

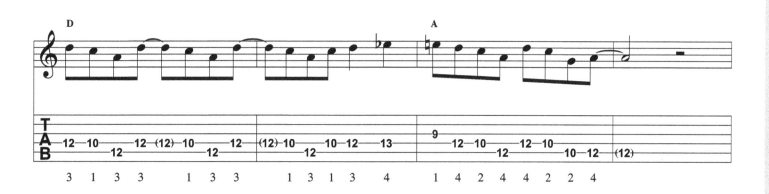

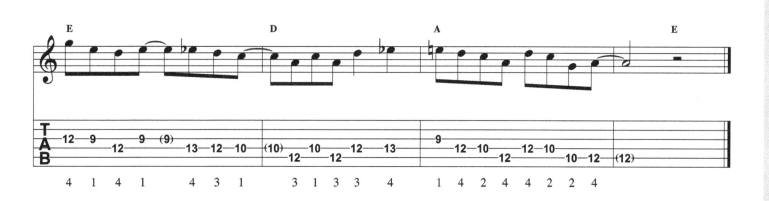

Multiple-Position Fingerings for A Minor Pentatonic and A Blues Scales

Below are examples of two-octave multiple-position fingerings for the A Minor Pentatonic and A Blues scales. In both of these examples, we begin in 9th position. As we ascend the scales, there are two shifts. The first shift is from 9th position to 12th position. The second shift occurs when we go from G on the 15th fret to A (the tonic) on the 17th fret; here, we move briefly from 12th position to 14th position. These shifts remain consistent as we descend through the scale. Pay close attention to the shifts, as this will help you play these scales cleanly and accurately.

13.15—A Minor Pentatonic Scale

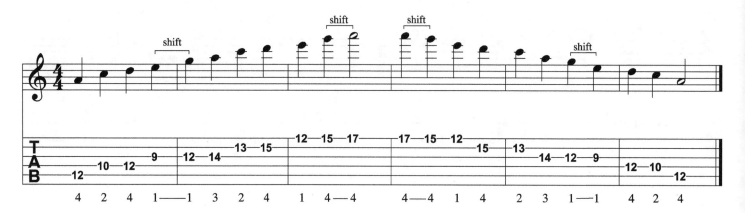

13.16—A Blues Scale

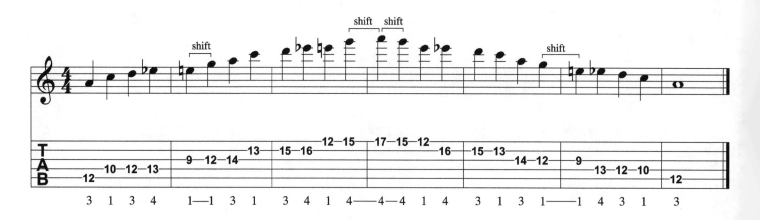

MULTIPLE-POSITION BLUES MELODY

Below is a blues melody written using a combination of the A Minor Pentatonic and A Blues scales. This example, which utilizes the scale fingerings from the previous page, begins in 9th position and goes all the way up to 14th position. Learning this melody will help reinforce the fingerings while introducing you to new blues ideas.

13.17

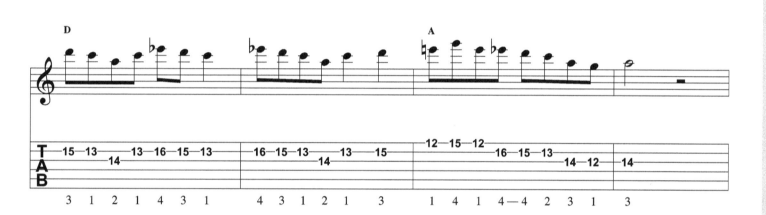

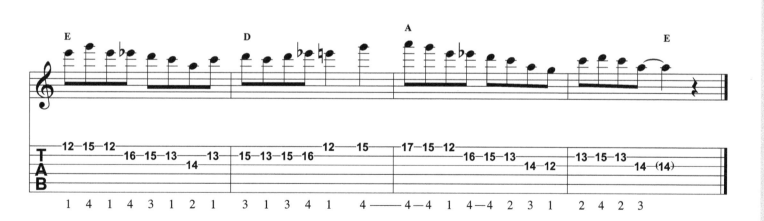

Unit 13 — Minor Pentatonic and Blues Scales—9th/10th Position and Multiple-Position Fingerings

Time Test 13

Write the fingering in the TAB for the following 9th-position blues idea.

Guitar Legends: Bonnie Raitt

Profile
- Born on November 8, 1949 in Burbank, California
- Daughter of actor John Raitt
- Began playing guitar at an early age
- Listed in *Rolling Stone* magazine among the "100 Greatest Guitarists"
- Also known for her political activism
- Inducted into the Rock and Roll Hall of Fame in 2000

Style
- Blends together blues, rock, folk, and country music
- Known as a bottleneck slide guitarist
- Integrates alternate tunings into her songs and her slide-guitar playing
- Plays the same $120 Stratocaster, called "Brownie," that she bought in 1969

Suggested Listening
- "Runaway"
- "Something to Talk About"
- "Pride and Joy"
- "Love Me Like a Man"

UNIT 14: COMMON FINGERINGS FOR SCALES AND CHORDS

OBJECTIVES

Upon completion of this unit, the student will:

- Know five common fingerings for the major scale
- Learn five common fingerings for the minor pentatonic scale
- Be able to play five common fingerings for the blues scale
- Know five common fingerings for major and minor triads
- Learn five common fingerings for the dominant 7th chord

Throughout this book, we have looked at various fingerings for the major scale, minor pentatonic scale, major triads, minor triads, minor 7th chords, and dominant 7th chords. You should now be able to see how the different shapes correspond throughout the various chords and scales, and how they can be moved to different keys. In this unit, we will review these fingerings and practice taking them into different key centers, moving up and down the neck.

MAJOR SCALE

14.1—The Five Common Fingerings for the Major Scale

These fingerings will remain intact no matter what key we are in. A scale can be played all the way up and down the fretboard by linking these fingerings together. For example, in C Major, we begin with Fingering 1 in open position and move up the fretboard (Fingerings 2, 3, 4, and 5) to play the scale up the neck (Example 14.2).

14.2—C Major Scale

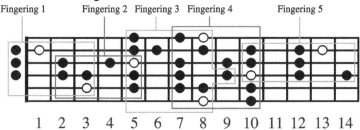

If we were in the key of F Major, we would begin with Fingering 4 in open position and continue up the neck in order (Fingerings 4, 5, 1, 2, and 3).

14.3—F Major Scale

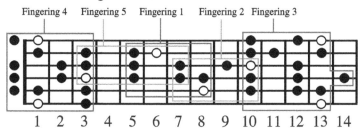

Common Fingerings for Scales and Chords ▪ Unit 14 135

The same is true for our five major-scale fingerings that include all the notes from the scale in a given position.

14.4

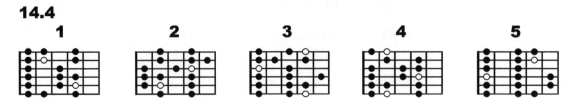

Assignments

1. Practice all of the fingerings on this page in the key of C Major.
2. Practice all of the fingerings on this page in the keys of F and G Major. Be sure to start with the fingering that is the lowest on the fretboard.
3. Pick three random sharp keys and three flat keys. Identify the fingering that corresponds to the lowest place on the fretboard that the scale can be played. From the lowest fingering, continue up the neck, progressing through the other fingerings in order.

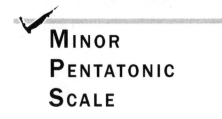

Minor Pentatonic Scale

As with the major scale on the previous page, the minor pentatonic scale follows a similar sequential order. Notice that the tonic notes on the fretboard (the white dots) are in the same place as in the major-scale fingerings.

14.5

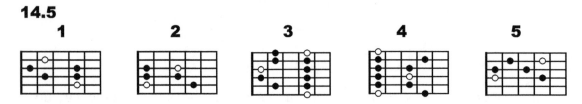

If our tonic note were C, the order would remain intact, beginning with Fingering 1 in open position and continuing sequentially (2, 3, 4, 5). The same is true when we look at the fingerings that include all the notes in a given position, as seen below.

14.6

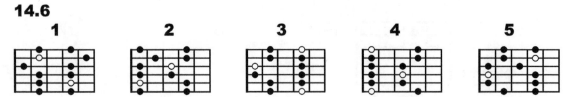

Assignments

1. Practice all of the fingerings on this page in A Minor Pentatonic.
2. Practice all of the fingerings on this page in D Minor Pentatonic and E Minor Pentatonic. Be sure to start with the fingering that is the lowest on the fretboard.
3. Pick three random sharp keys and three flat keys. Identify the fingering that corresponds to the lowest place on the fretboard that the scale can be played. From the lowest fingering, continue up the neck, progressing through the other fingerings in order.

✓ THE BLUES SCALE

The blues scale follows an identical sequential order to the minor pentatonic scale. Remember, the blues scale has only has one different note from the corresponding minor pentatonic scale. As you go through the fingerings below, be mindful once again of the octave shapes of the tonic notes on the fretboard.

14.7

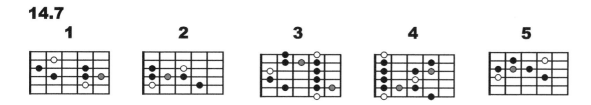

Like we saw with the fingerings of the minor pentatonic scale on the previous page, if our tonic note were C, the order would remain intact—beginning with fingering 1 in open position and continuing sequentially (2, 3, 4, 5). This is also true when we look at the fingerings that include all the notes of the blues scale in a given position, as seen below.

14.8

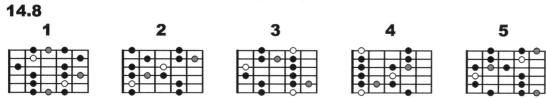

Assignments

1. Practice all of the fingerings on this page in A Blues.
2. Practice all of the fingerings on this page in D Blues and E Blues. Be sure to start with the fingering that is the lowest on the fretboard.
3. Pick three random sharp keys and three flat keys. Identify the fingering that corresponds to the lowest place on the fretboard that the scale can be played. From the lowest fingering, continue up the neck, progressing through the other fingerings in order.

✓ MAJOR TRIADS

Below are fingerings for the root-position major triad moving up the fretboard. These shapes are moveable and follow the same sequential order we've seen throughout this chapter. Notice once again how the octave shapes of the tonic notes on the fretboard are the same as with the scales already covered.

14.9

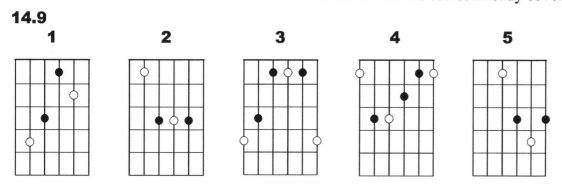

Common Fingerings for Scales and Chords ■ Unit 14 137

If we were to play the C Major triad up the neck of the guitar, we would begin with Fingering 1 in open position. From there, we would continue up the neck in sequential order (2, 3, 4, 5).

14.10—C Major Triads

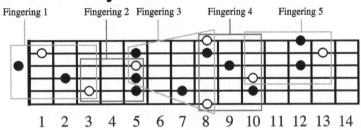

Assignment

1. Practice all the fingerings above as a C Major chord.
2. Practice all the fingerings above as F Major and G Major chords. Be sure to start with the fingering that is the lowest on the fretboard.
3. Pick three random major chords. Identify the fingering that corresponds to the lowest place on the fretboard that the chord can be played. From the lowest fingering, continue up the neck, progressing through the other fingerings in order.

Minor Triads

Below are fingerings for the root-position minor triad as it moves up the neck. Once again, we have shapes that move in sequential order. Be mindful of the octave shapes of the tonic notes as they ascend the fretboard.

14.11

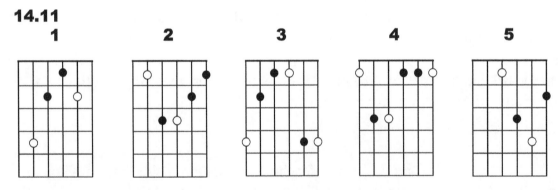

Assignment

1. Practice all the fingerings above as an A Minor chord.
2. Practice all the fingerings above as D Minor and E Minor chords. Be sure to start with the fingering that is the lowest on the fretboard.
3. Pick three random minor chords. Identify the fingering that corresponds to the lowest place on the fretboard that the chord can be played. From the lowest fingering, continue up the neck, progressing through the other fingerings in order.

Dominant 7th Chords

In Unit 8, we introduced the concept of the dominant 7th chord. Please review the construction of that chord for further enrichment. In that unit, we looked at the chords derived from the corresponding major-triad barre-chord fingerings. Below are the fingerings that come out of each of the five shapes we have been looking at in this unit.

14.12

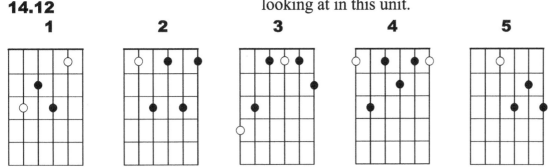

If we were to play these fingerings as a C7 chord, we would start with fingering 1 in 1st position. From there, we would continue up the neck in sequential order (2, 3, 4, 5).

Assignment
1. Practice all the fingerings above as a C7 chord.
2. Practice all the fingerings above as F7 and G7 chords. Be sure to start with the fingering that is the lowest on the fretboard.
3. Pick three random dominant 7th chords. Identify the fingering that corresponds to the lowest place on the fretboard that the chord can be played. From the lowest fingering, continue up the neck, progressing through the other fingerings in order.

Minor 7th Chords

Below are fingerings of the minor 7th chord that come out of the five shapes we have been looking at in this chapter. Notice the similarities between these fingerings and the related minor-triad fingerings on page 138.

14.13

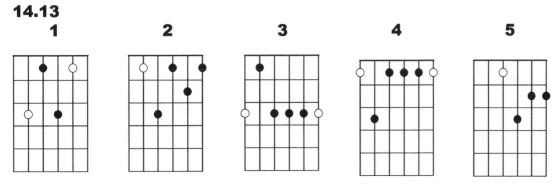

Assignment
1. Practice all the fingerings above as a Cmin7 chord.
2. Practice all the fingerings above as Fmin7 and Gmin7 chords. Be sure to start with the fingering that is the lowest on the fretboard.
3. Pick three random minor 7th chords. Identify the fingering that corresponds to the lowest place on the fretboard that the chord can be played. From the lowest fingering, continue up the neck, progressing through the other fingerings in order.

Chords and Songs

UNIT 15: CHORDS AND SONGS

In this section of the book, you will be introduced to a variety of songs from many different genres. All of these songs will build upon skills covered in this volume, as well as in Book 1. The songs increase in complexity as you progress through the unit. You will begin by learning songs that combine open chords learned in Book 1 with barre chords. From there, you will work on songs with power chords and barre chords. As you near the end of this unit, you will combine all of this and learn some classic rock tunes and riffs.

When learning these songs, it is important to have a strategy for digesting the music in a comprehensive way. Below are 10 concepts to be aware of as you approach each of the following tunes.

1. **Go slowly.** If you learn aspects of these tunes correctly at a slow tempo, your chances of playing the song at the desired tempo will greatly increase.
2. **Break down the piece into short phrases.** In learning a piece phrase by phrase, you will approach it more musically and organically. From there, you can progress to playing one section at a time and, eventually, work on putting it all together to play the piece in its entirety.
3. **Practice in time.** Use a metronome to help you develop a good internal sense of time.
4. **Listen to the original recording.** By listening to an original recording of the song you are working on, you will notice how close you are to getting the sound of the tune and, hopefully, become inspired to finish it.
5. **Isolate.** If there is a part of a song that is challenging, isolate that part. Play it very slowly out of time. As you become accustomed to the mechanics of the tune, you can start to play it in time—*slowly* at first, until you get it to performance tempo.
6. **Record yourself.** This is the quickest way to grow on the instrument. Ultimately, you should know what the song should sound like. Recording yourself will always give you an accurate account of where you are. It can be hard to take sometimes, but with consistency, it will help you become a better guitarist.
7. **Pay attention.** If there are specific fingerings indicated, be aware of those fingerings. These will help you in the long run. A fingering of your own—isolated—might feel more comfortable than the one presented, but when you have to start changing to other fingerings, you will realize there is a reason why one fingering is favored over another.
8. **Jam.** If you are playing these songs in a class, get together with your colleagues to play the music together. This creates camaraderie, and you might just learn something from your fellow students.
9. **Repetition is the mother of all skill.** When you are practicing a section and have learned it, repeat it multiple times. By doing so, you are programming your musical consciousness to really absorb the song. Try playing it multiple times without mistakes. That's how you really learn a skill or song.
10. **Journal.** A practice journal where you record what you accomplish each day is very important. It helps to focus your practice sessions and documents your journey and growth on the instrument.

John Denver: Take Me Home, Country Roads

Chords Used

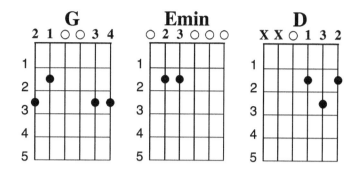

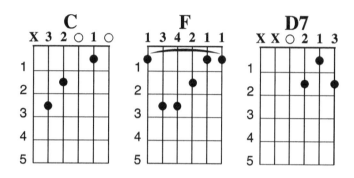

Strumming Pattern

While you can play this tune in any key by using a capo, the strumming pattern is illustrated with a G chord for clarity.

Swing

Tips for Playing This Song

- The original key for this song is A Major. In order to play it in that key using the chord forms above, you need to capo the 2nd fret. If you are singing this song, you can place the capo anywhere on the fretboard that suits your vocal range.
- Practice the strumming pattern slowly for accuracy. You want to make sure you are able to keep this rhythm going comfortably throughout the song.
- To vary the pattern, you can alternate between the root of the chord on beat 1 and a different note of the chord—on an adjacent string—on beat 3.
- Practice in sections by isolating the verse, chorus, and bridge.

Lou Reed: Walk on the Wild Side

Chords Used

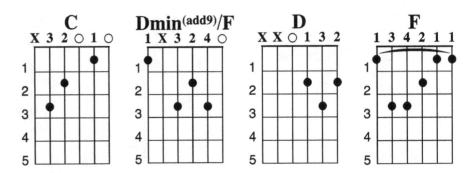

Strumming Patterns

Below are two patterns you can use with this song.

No. 1

No. 2

Tips for Playing This Song

- At first, practice getting the rhythm down using just one chord. Once you are able to do that, move to two chords. Then, put together the song.
- Practice the strumming rhythm slowly for accuracy. You want to make sure you are able to keep this rhythm going comfortably throughout the duration of the song.
- Experiment with varying the pattern somewhat while maintaining the basic feel.
- The guitar part is subtle in this piece but important to the overall feel.

R.E.M.: Losing My Religion

Chords Used

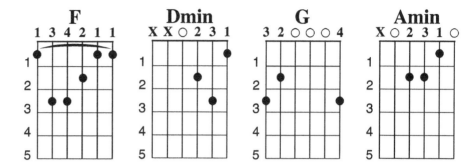
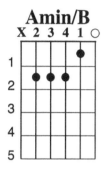
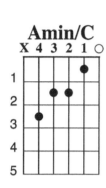
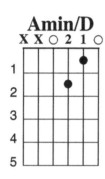
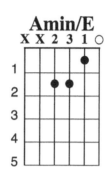
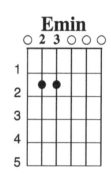
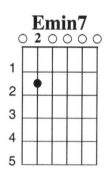

Strumming Pattern

Below is a basic strumming pattern you can use for this song.

Tips for Playing This Song

- Practice this strumming pattern with just one chord. Pay close attention to the choke strum and the two-measure rhythm. Once you are comfortable playing the pattern with one chord, move to two chords. Then, put the entire song together.
- Practice the strumming rhythm slowly for accuracy. Be certain you are able to keep this rhythm going comfortably throughout the duration of the song.
- Experiment with varying the pattern somewhat while maintaining the basic feel.

Unit 15 — Chords and Songs 143

The Who: Baba O'Riley

Chords Used

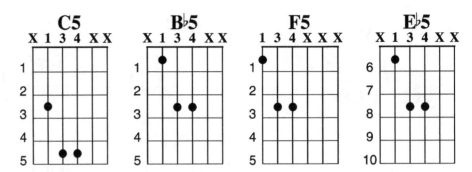

The following chords are for the end and are played Capo III:

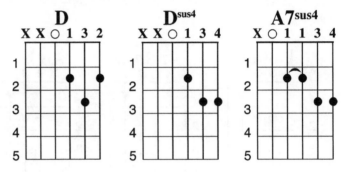

Strumming Pattern

This is the basic rhythm-guitar part for most of the song.

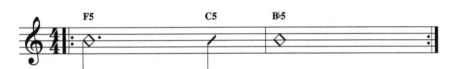

Tips for Playing This Song

- The rhythm-guitar part above is played through most of the song. There are, however, some different rhythms that occur later in the song. Practice getting the first rhythm-guitar part down before trying to learn those other parts.
- Make sure your power chords are sustaining and ringing out clearly.
- There are multiple guitar parts in this song, but the strumming pattern above shows the main part.
- The chords in the second row at the top of the page are for the ending instrumental section. They should be played with a capo at the 3rd fret.

THE WHO: BEHIND BLUE EYES

Chords Used

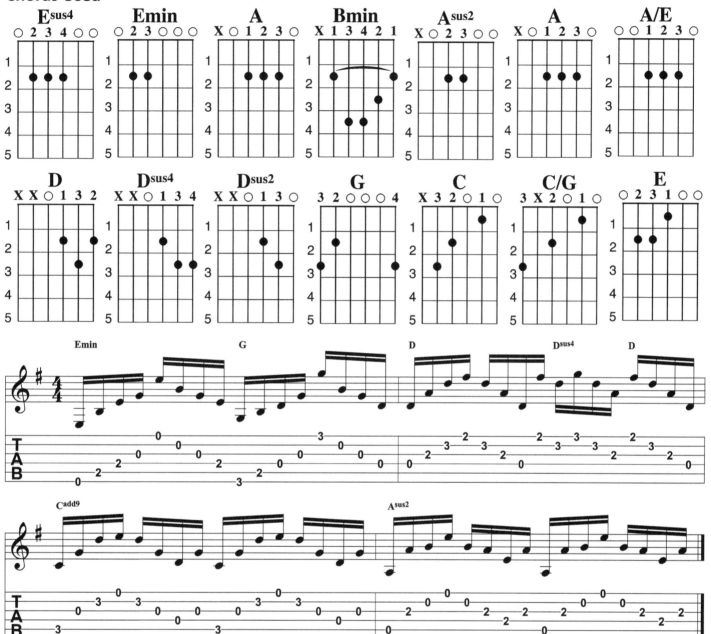

Strumming Pattern

The pattern on the right can be used and applied in the appropriate sections with variations.

TIPS FOR PLAYING THIS SONG

- Learn the fingerstyle and strumming patterns above. You can start with these and then experiment with your own variations as you play the song.
- Play along with the original recording so you can capture the feel of the song.
- Practice the chord changes slowly and accurately.

Unit 15   Chords and Songs   145

Green Day: Brain Stew

Chords Used

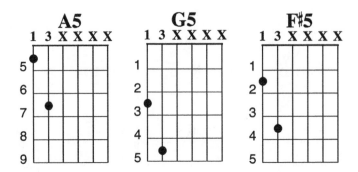

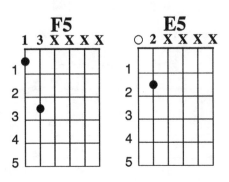

Strumming Patterns

Below are two strumming patterns used in different sections of the tune.

No. 1

No. 2

Tips for Playing This Song

- The original recording of this song is played with the guitars tuned down one half step. If playing with the recording, you'll notice that the chords don't match up. We have kept it in standard tuning for ease of playing. If you feel so inclined, you can try to tune your guitar down one half step to play with the recording. The same chord voicings will be played in the same positions.
- All of these chords should be played with downstrokes.
- Be aware of the two different rhythm-guitar parts and note when each one is played.
- Be mindful of the choke strums in the second strumming pattern.

The Rolling Stones: Everybody Needs Somebody to Love

Chords Used

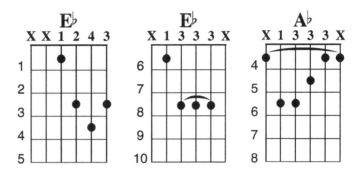

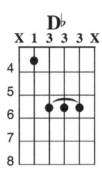 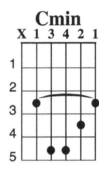 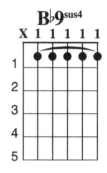 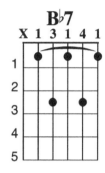

Strumming Pattern

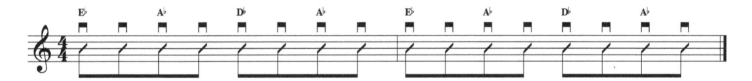

Tips for Playing This Song

- The majority of this song contains three chords (E♭, A♭, and D♭) played E♭–A♭–D♭–A♭. You can play this with all barre chords, or you can use the E♭ chord in 1st position.
- All chords in the strumming pattern above should be played with downstrokes.
- Practice along with the recording.
- As you begin to learn this progression, you may start to develop some fatigue in your hand. This is just a matter of endurance—but don't play through the pain. With repetition, you will be able to develop the endurance necessary to play this song for a long time.

Green Day: Holiday

Chords Used

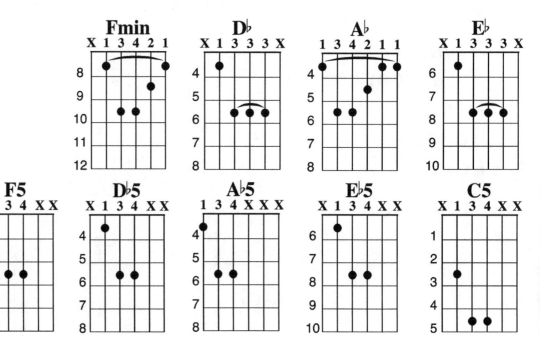

Strumming Patterns

Below are three strumming patterns that can be used with this song. The two rows of chords represent two different options for you to experiment with.

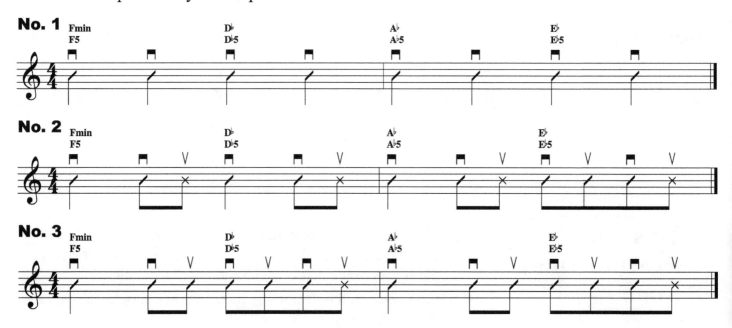

Tips for Playing This Song

- Practice this song using both the full barre chords listed above, as well as the power chords.
- When first practicing this song, play it using straight quarter notes as shown in the first strumming pattern.
- The second strumming pattern is for the verse while the third is for the chorus. These are basic rhythms that you can vary as you play the song.
- Make sure you practice the choke strum and play it correctly in rhythm.
- Practice with the original recording.

148   Chords and Songs   Unit 15

The Rolling Stones: Midnight Rambler

Chords Used

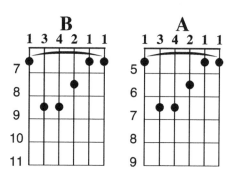
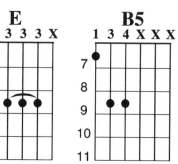
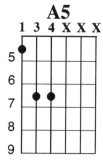
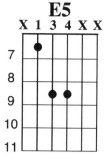

Strumming Patterns

Below are three strumming patterns you can use in this song. In the first pattern, the two rows of chords represent two options for you to try.

No. 1

No. 2

No. 3

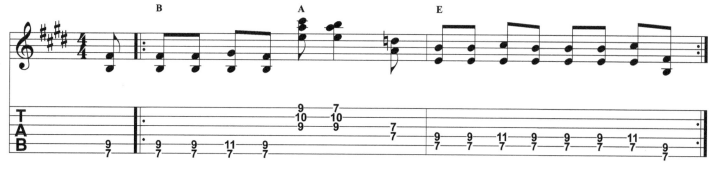

Tips for Playing This Song

- Practice this song using both the full barre chords shown above, as well as the power chords.
- The eighth-note rhythm is played with a swing feel, as opposed to straight.
- Because there are only three chords in this song, you can use any or all of the above patterns, as well as variations, to play the song.
- Practice with the recording.

Unit 15 ■ Chords and Songs

Sheryl Crow: Soak Up the Sun

Chords Used

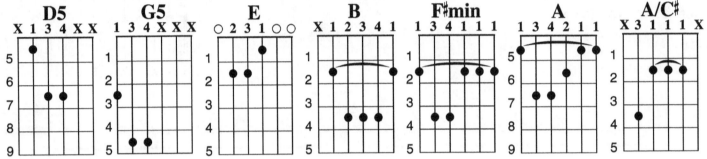

Strumming Patterns

Intro/Verse

Bridge

Chorus

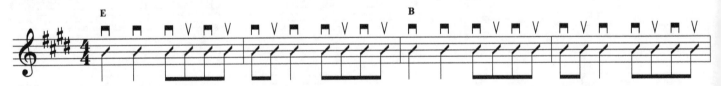

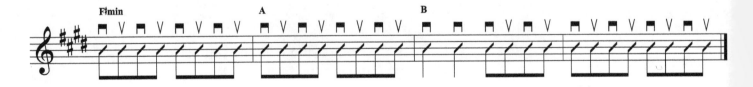

Tips for Playing This Song

- All three basic sections of the tune are presented above. Practice each one slowly for accuracy.
- Practice along with the original recording.

Eagles: Desperado

Chords Used

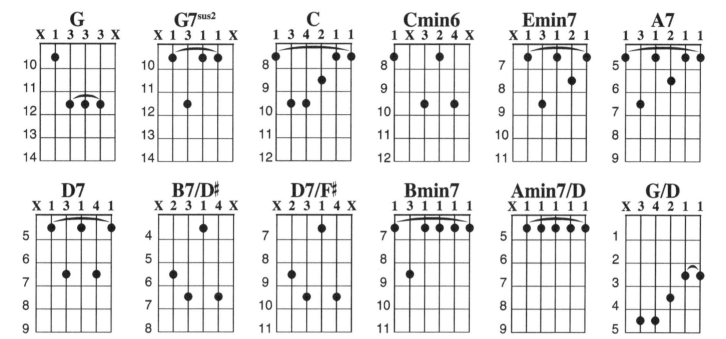

Strumming Pattern

Tips for Playing This Song

- Concentrate on seamless transitions between the barre chords.
- A steady quarter-note strumming pattern can be used throughout this song but especially in the beginning. As you become more familiar with the song and move on into the chorus, you can experiment with other strumming patterns that give the song a bit more motion.
- Feel free to practice this song using other chord voicings than those presented. You can even integrate those chords into your performance along with the ones shown above.
- Practice along with the original recording.

CHICAGO: 25 OR 6 TO 4

Chords Used

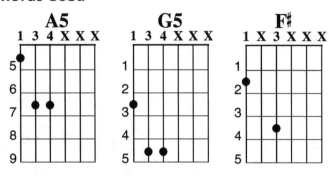

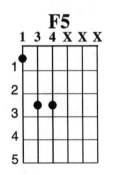 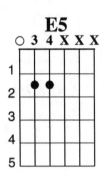 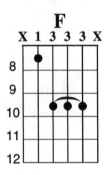 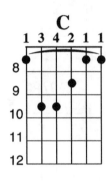 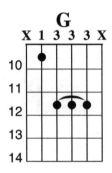

Strumming Pattern
Intro and Verse

Chorus

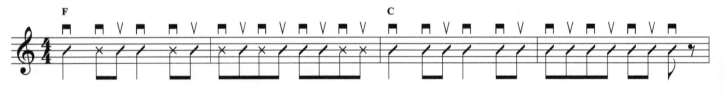

TIPS FOR PLAYING THIS SONG

- This song contains many different layers, but the two sections above will give you the sound and feel of the song.
- When playing the F♯, play it as an octave sound as indicated in the chord diagram. This will prevent clashes with the actual chord played there by other parts of the band while still giving you the feel of the song.
- The strumming pattern for the chorus can be varied. Be aware of the choke strums, as these will produce the desired percussive effect for the song.
- Practice along with the original recording.

Improvisation

UNIT 16: IMPROVISATION

IMPROVISATION USING THE MAJOR SCALE

In this section, we are going to begin improvising using some of the scales covered in this book. For purposes of discussion, we are going to address improvisation from a diatonic perspective. To do this, we need to look at the chords generated off of each of the degrees of the major scale.

When we build triads off of each degree of the C Major scale, we get the following chords.

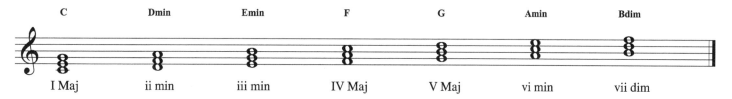

This is important information to grasp, as it will help you understand chord progressions. Triads built off of each degree of the major scale are the same, regardless of what key you are in. For the key of C, we get the chords that are listed above the staff in each position of the scale. The chords listed below the staff represent the diatonic triad qualities for the major scale. These qualities are consistent regardless of what key you are playing. For example, if you were to look at the key of G Major, you would get the following diatonic chords.

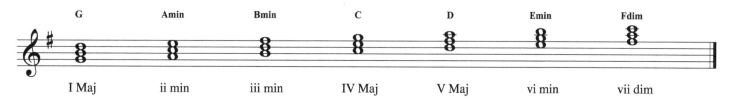

You'll notice that the chord qualities remained consistent in each position. Therefore, if we take a look at the following progression, we notice that this chord progression is a diatonic progression in the key of G Major. The chord progression can be expressed with Roman numerals as: I–IV–I–V. This comes from a centuries-old system for identifying relationships between chords in a given piece of music.

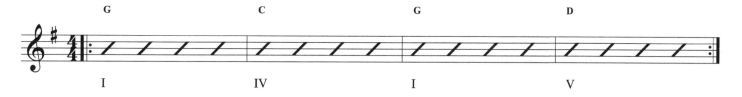

Because all of the chords in the above progression are diatonic to the key of G Major, you can use the G Major scale to improvise over that progression.

While practicing this in class, try to alternate between improvising and playing chords.

Identify the key and label each chord with the appropriate Roman numeral for the following progressions. Practice improvising using the appropriate major scale for each progression.

No. 1

Key:

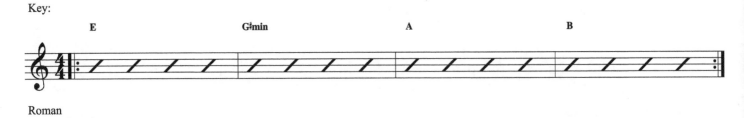

Roman Numeral:

No. 2

Key:

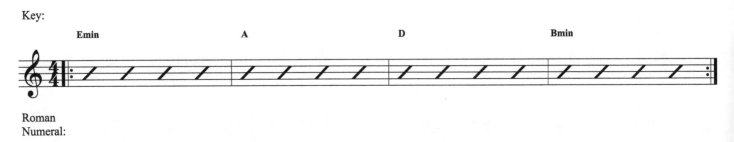

Roman Numeral:

No. 3

Key:

Roman Numeral:

No. 4

Key:

Roman Numeral:

Improvisation Using the Minor Pentatonic Scale

Throughout the book, we have looked at applying the minor pentatonic scale over a blues progression. We have also looked at the minor 7th chord and dominant 7th chord. The minor 7th chord consists of: root–♭3rd–5th–♭7th. The dominant 7th chord consists of: root–3rd–5th–♭7th.

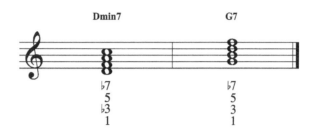

The minor pentatonic scale is made up of: root–♭3rd–4th–5th–♭7th.

If we compare the Dmin7 chord to the D Minor Pentatonic scale, we see that the four notes of the Dmin7 chord are found in the D Minor Pentatonic scale. We can also see that two of the four notes in the G7 chord are also found in the D Minor Pentatonic scale. All of these notes are also consistent with the key of C Major, as Dmin7–G7 is a ii–V progression in the key of C Major. (Note the Roman numeral analysis for the C Major scale below.)

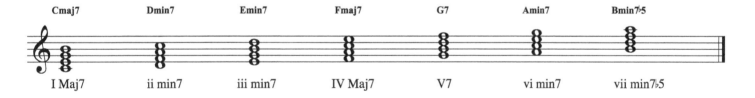

Because of this, we can use the minor pentatonic scale with the root of the ii chord to play over a ii–V progression. In the progression below, we have a ii–V progression with a Dmin7 and G7 chord. Practice using the D Minor Pentatonic scale to improvise over this progression.

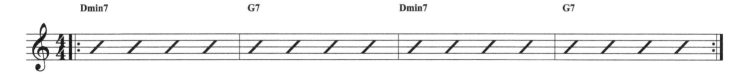

Unit 16   Improvisation 155

You can also play the minor pentatonic scale over a static minor 7th chord. Practice soloing over an Fmin7 chord using the F Minor Pentatonic scale.

You could also use the minor pentatonic scale to solo over a static dominant 7th chord. On the previous page, we saw how we could play a D Minor Pentatonic scale over a G7 chord. The note D is the 5th of the G7 chord. Therefore, we could play a minor pentatonic scale built off the 5th degree of any dominant 7th chord. Below is a static C7 chord. The 5th of that chord is G. Practice soloing over a C7 chord using the G Minor Pentatonic scale.

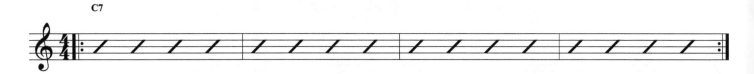

You can also use the minor pentatonic scale to play over progressions built out of a minor key. Below are the diatonic chords for the key of A Minor.

Key of A Minor

Just like the major key, the order and quality of chords in a minor key remain consistent as you take the formula above to other keys.

Below is a progression in the key of A Minor. Notice how this relates to the diatonic harmony presented above. Practice soloing over this progression using the A Minor Pentatonic scale.

Combining the Major Scale and Minor Pentatonic Scale in Improvisation

Now, let's look at how we can combine scales when improvising. Below is a 16-measure progression. Notice that the example is a series of ii–V–I progressions in three different keys. The first system consists of Emin7–A7–D, which is a ii–V–I progression in the key of D. You could improvise over this progression two different ways. Because the chords are all in the key of D Major, you can use the D Major scale to solo over those four measures. Another option is to use an E Minor Pentatonic scale over the Emin and A7 chords and then switch to a D Major scale when you arrive at the D chord. This will give your improvisation a different sound and color. You would continue this type of application through the rest of the song. In the example below, both approaches are presented. Practice improvising over this progression, and use both methods so you can better reinforce the material.

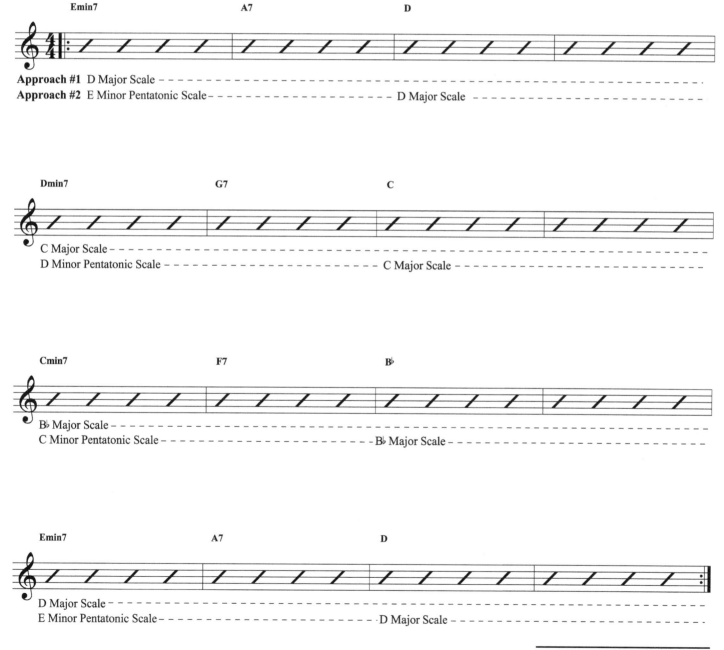

Time Test Answers

Page Answers

13 **Time Test 1: No. 1**

13 **Time Test 1: No. 2**

24 **Time Test 2**

35 **Time Test 3**

A Minor Pentatonic Scale

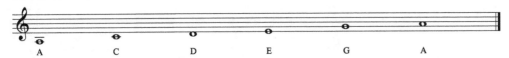

A Blues Scale

44 **Time Test 4**

G–Cmin–B♭–F–C
Amin–E♭–Dmin–Fmin–Bmin

54 **Time Test 5**

A5–C5–G5–B5–F5
E5–B♭5/F–D5–A♭5–B♭5

63 **Time Test 6**

(performance)

Page Answers

75 **Time Test 7**

84 **Time Test 8**

G–Emin–F7–Bmin7
Dmin–B–Gmin7–A7

94 **Time Test 9**

Amin–Dmin–F–E
A7–D7–E7–Emin7

105 **Time Test 10**

114 **Time Test 11**

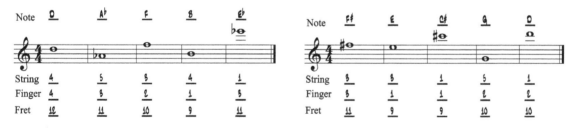

125 **Time Test 12**

134 **Time Test 13**

Common Fingerings

Major Scale

Minor Pentatonic Scale

Blues Scale

Major Triads

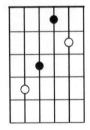 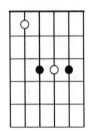 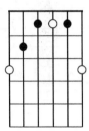 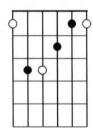 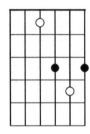

Minor Triads

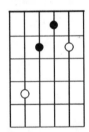 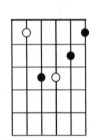 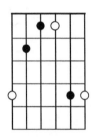 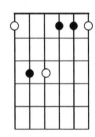 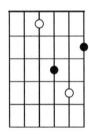

Minor 7th Chords

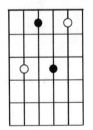 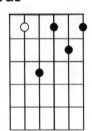 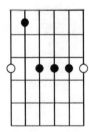 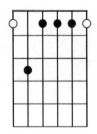 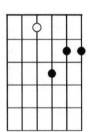

Dominant 7th Chords

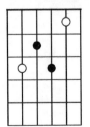 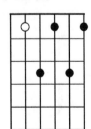 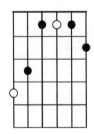 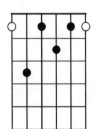 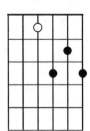